W9-BCF-900

THE SIMPLE STEPS TO GOD

The Simple Steps to God

+

by

FATHER FRANÇOIS
of Saint Mary, O.C.D.

Copy 1

DIMENSION BOOKS

WILKES-BARRE, PENNSYLVANIA

Published by Dimension Books
Wilkes-Barre, Pennsylvania

This is a translation of *Présence à Dieu et à soi-même* by Reverend Father François de Sainte Marie, O.C.D. (Paris: Editions du Seuil, 1943. This English version has been made from the sixth French edition. The Translator is Harold Evans.

Library of Congress Catalog Card Number: 63-20361

First Edition © 1943 by Editions du Seuil

Nihil Obstat

Rev. James F. Smurl, S.T.D.
  Censor Librorum
July 1st, 1963

Imprimatur

✠ Jerome D. Hannon
  Bishop of Scranton
July 3rd, 1963

For permission to make brief quotations from the following books, grateful acknowledgement is hereby made to the holders of the original copyrights: *The Complete Works of Saint Teresa of Jesus*, translated and edited by E. Allison Peers from the critical edition of P. Silverio de Santa Teresa, O.C.D., New York: Sheed & Ward, 1957; *The Complete Works of Saint John of the Cross*, translated and edited by E. Allison Peers from the critical edition of P. Silverio de Santa Teresa, O.C.D., Westminster, Md.: The Newman Press, 1957; *Practice of the Presence of God*, translated by Sister Mary David, S.S.N.D., Westminster, Md.: The Newman Press, 1957; *The Cross of Jesus* by Louis Chardon, O.P., St. Louis: B. Herder Book Co., 1959; *Seraph Among Angels: The Life of St. Mary Magdalene de' Pazzi*, by Sister Mary Minima, Chicago: The Carmelite Press, 1958; *The Spiritual Doctrine of Sister Elizabeth of the Trinity* by M. M. Philipon, O.P., Westminster, Md., The Newman Press, 1961; and *Autobiography of Saint Thérèse of Lisieux*, New York: P. J. Kenedy & Sons, 1958.

VOLUME ONE

The Carmel Series on Christian Life

Under the Direction of Father Kieran Kavanaugh, O.C.D.

Contents

Introduction

THE Carmelite tradition is sometimes con-
trasted with that of the Benedictines and even
set in opposition to it: as if Benedictine piety were
liturgical and objective and Carmelite spirituality
individualistic and subjective. On the basis of this
oversimplified distinction, partisans can line up in
opposing factions and argue with one another about
the relative merits of the two "schools." It is inevit-
able that such divisions should spring into existence
but we must regret them, for they diminish the
horizons of the Christian spirit. In actual fact, both
the Carmelites and the Benedictines of our day
can and should appeal to a common monastic tradition with its roots in the Oriental Desert spirituality. If the Benedictines have maintained the

emphasis on community and liturgy, the Carmelites are no less traditional in their emphasis on solitude and contemplative prayer. These two trends, far from being opposed to one another, actually complement one another. Without both these emphases the monastic spiritual tradition is incomplete.

It is true that the Carmelites are now "friars" (mendicants) rather than "monks," but their original sources, the hermit communities of Mount Carmel in the 12th century, were purely and authentically "monastic." The spirit of Carmel has always been nourished by these monastic roots. And a monk is one whose whole life is summed up in the search for God. *Si revera Deum quaerit,* says the Rule of St. Benedict.

One who seeks God seeks the supreme, though invisible Reality. He therefore exposes his whole life to anguish and to risk. He seeks supreme security in what seems to the world supremely insecure. How can he ever be "sure" that he is seeking God, and much more, how can he ever be sure that he has "found" Him?

Christ prayed at the Last Supper that His Apostles might be "sanctified in truth." The word of God is truth, the highest reality, planted in the depths of our being by our Creator and Redeemer. This word must grow in us like a seed. It must awaken to life, to knowledge, to love, to experience. Our whole interior life is centered on the spiritual "activity" and "dynamism" of this word which St. Paul calls "living and efficacious." The efficacy of the word of God in us depends on faith, and our faith is itself a gift of God. The "living and efficacious" word of God, received by faith, fully embraced by loving acceptance in the depths of our being, flowers into an experience of God as present to us. We come, in this experience of presence, to an inexplicable, yet utterly real, personal awareness of the Almighty Who loves us and dwells in our inmost heart.

To reach this spiritual awareness of God, this "knowledge" of God in the obscurity of faith, we must first of all awaken to a knowledge of our true selves. And so we must pray, as did Saint Augustine: "Lord, let me know myself and let me know Thee." If we do not know ourselves, we cannot know God either. But we must know ourselves rightly, as images of God. And so we must avoid a twofold danger. On one hand we tend to indulge in unhealthy introspection, analyzing ourselves without end. On the other, ignoring the reality both of ourselves and God, we tend to take God for granted and to assume that He is simply what we want Him to be. Instead of knowing ourselves as images of God, we contemplate a god who is the image of ourselves. That means our "god" is an idol—the justification of our own illusion about ourselves. Under such conditions, the interior life is anything but real.

Father François of Saint Mary is a Carmelite, and speaks for the austere and simple Carmelite tradition. One may therefore expect to read in these pages a message that has something in it of an austerity and truth that cannot be found except in the desert. Yet, since the author is also a spiritual son of the gracious Saint Teresa of Avila, we may also expect to find that the "spirit and power of Elias" it here tempered by a charming humanism. The combination of austerity and kindness, detachment and good humor, mysticism and common sense, is one of the characteristics of Carmel. All these qualities will be found in this little treatise.

This volume originated in certain spiritual conferences addressed to a group of French lay people during the German occupation of Paris. I mention this not because the war enters into Father François' discussion of the spiritual life, but in order to remind the reader that the book is one of the fruits of a notable spiritual harvest that began in France in the darkest days of her history and which is by now nourishing the whole Christian world. One wonders when the hunger for the interior life which so many Americans are beginning to feel, will be satisfied by "Schools of Mental Prayer" like the one in which those talks were given. May the example of Father François inspire the zeal of our English and American Carmelites to share with their compatriots the message and the experience of Saint Teresa and Saint John of the Cross.

Living in the truth, the reality of our own being, the reality of God, our union with God in prayer, and the deep spiritual value of our ordinary every day life when it is supernaturalized by faith: such

are the subjects dealt with in these pages. Father
François draws so plentifully upon the tradition
of his order that his treatment of these themes
make up a clear summary of the theology of the interior life as it is taught by the great mystics of
Carmel. But the chief value of this treatise is that
it offers nothing too lofty or too obscure for the
ordinary Christian to understand. It is a handbook
of the spiritual life excellent for married people
in the world, as well as religious in their cloister.
All will doubtless be grateful for it, and will keep
it within easy reach, returning over and over again
to the thoughtful perusal of its wholesome message. I, who write these words, would not be writing them if I had not myself profited, in meditation,
by the wisdom and simplicity which Father François has been so kind as to share with his brothers
in Christ. That is why I am happy to preface his
volume with these words of sincere appreciation.

May this book awaken many good souls from the
confusion of a "spiritual" life that has been hitherto
without spirit, and bring them face to face with
themselves and with God. May it show them the
way to find Him in silence and faith, in self-sacri-

fice and ardent charity. May it give glory to the God of heaven by teaching men how infinitely worthy He is of all the love of their hearts, and may it reveal to their souls the secret ways of pure prayer.

THOMAS MERTON
(Fr. M. Louis, O.C.S.O.)
Abbey of Gethsemani

THE SIMPLE STEPS TO GOD

1

Walking In The Truth

GOOD sense and sound judgment, by which are meant the practical use of our thinking faculties, bring us to see things as they really are, as they exist in the world around us. It goes without saying that there can be no perfection of the soul without them. They are, so to speak, the groundwork of perfection, matters of the first importance.

St. Teresa, whose views in this matter are universally acknowledged to be right, had no wish to have people in her convents who were too limited in these areas, and for this reason: with them there is little hope of any spiritual progress being made. "If a person is going to reform himself" she says, "and to advance in virtue, then he must first of all be a person of intelligence, of sound judgment." [1]

St. John of the Cross takes the same view. "Enter into account with thy reason", he writes in his *Maxims*. "He that acts according to reason is like one that eats of substantial food." [2]

In one way or another all Carmelite spiritual writers give evidence of this same fundamental confidence in reason which joins the life of devotion to natural realities in the same way that a healthy vine-stock is rooted in the soil which nourishes and feeds it. And in this attitude they take toward reason we already have the rough sketch of their whole philosophy of the spiritual life.

Nevertheless, above and beyond the light of reason, there is the more brilliant sun of faith.

[1] *Way of Perfection*, Chapter XIV, *Complete works of Saint Teresa of Jesus* (3 vols.), translated and edited by E. Allison Peers from the critical edition of P. Silverio de Santa Teresa, O.C.D. (New York: Sheed & Ward, 1957), Vol. II, p. 57.

[2] *Spiritual Sentences and Maxims*, n. 41 and n. 43. *The Complete Works of St. John of the Cross* (3 vols.), translated and edited by E. Allison Peers from the critical edition of P. Sil-

In the light of faith, another Reality—An Infinite Reality—is indissolubly linked with the realities we already know by reason. This is the Reality of God —"He Who is." This is that "sea of glass, like unto crystal" (Apocalypse 4:6) which stretches farther than the eye can see before the throne of God.

Through faith and reason joined to one another in this way, the Christian has a kind of super- natural good sense which leads him to see things as they are actually seen by God, to see them as they truly are. A spiritual life which is at all serious thus become a continuous effort to be true, to see all circumstances in proportion and perspective— with an eye made clear by purity of intention, with a glance enlightened by supernatural faith.

The mystic life is nothing other than the fuller development, the flowering, of this supernatural realism. Have not pure souls, or those at least who wish to become such, heard directly God's call inviting them to be true to themselves in fulfillment of the law of love?

verio de Santa Teresa, O.C.D. (third revised edition, West- minster, Md.: The Newman Press, 1957), Vol. III, p. 223.

One thinks in this connection of Psichari who, on returning to the Catholic faith, wrote in his diary: "Now, and from now on, for me at least, it is simply a matter of my being logical." Even the so-called "irrational" elements of the interior life—the obscurities, the mysterious purifications and trials—have just one objective, that the soul may be snatched by main force from attachment to half-truths and be directed through painstaking effort to see things as they really are: on the one hand, its own unworthiness as a creature, and on the other the infinite goodness and greatness of God. Thus the spiritual adventure described by St. John of the Cross under the figure of an escape at night is by no means an act of imprudence or foolishness: it is a fully reasonable undertaking whose object is to release the soul from its attachments, to set it free from them.

But it is difficult, and at times seems impossible, to be truthful to such an heroic degree.

In the natural order all we have to do is to open our eyes to see what is clearly before us, though even here prejudice and passion get in our way. In the spiritual life, the possibilities of error are

WALKING IN THE TRUTH

greater. It is difficult to see things clearly, for both concupiscence and the imagination join in leading us away from reality.

As a result, temptation and sin conspire to draw us from God.

Temptation may be described as a condition in which we are inclined to see things other than God has made them, outside the framework of moral and supernatural law according to which they may justly be enjoyed. In our misguided state we look at them from another point of view: as Satan, the father of lies and illusion, would have us see them. In consequence, things become sources of error to us. They become incitements to evil and to untruth. Then, after a moment of feverish curiosity, the eyes of those who wish "to become like unto God" are opened again; a renewed sense of reality dawns harshly upon us. Like Eve in the Garden of Eden, we at last recognize our mistake and sigh: "It was the serpent who deceived me." (Genesis 3:13).

But Satan continues to deceive us by making use of all those powerful forces in us which have drawn men away from the truth ever since the

Fall. "Sin is the illusion which I wish you to fear above all other things," wrote St. Teresa. The paths of life may be compared to those of a desert; as we wander through them, all at once we imagine that we see something. But it is a mirage, an oasis that is just a fantasy and it is foolish of us to think we can rest and enjoy ourselves there. The traveler who succumbs to its temptation cannot escape being unhappy, for he soon loses his way. The vision quickly fades and he finds himself in a path even darker and bleaker than it had been before. After a brief moment of allurement, the sinner sadly experiences a rude jolt back to the reality he had chosen to ignore for a time, and which now takes its full revenge upon him.

In contrast, let us admire and imitate the attitude of Christ when he was tempted. Against the charms of the Devil he defended himself by recourse to the truth; appealing with stern objectivity to the words of Scripture, he utterly smashed the efforts of his adversary, giving us an example in the fullest fashion possible of whole-hearted adherence to the truth.

The play of the imagination, even when it does not lead us into actual sin, may easily put us on the fringe of reality unless we are most careful. In its ordinary functioning, the imagination tends to draw us from the center of reality, to take us from the straight and narrow path which leads to holiness. In it lies the need for that diversion and distraction that greatly troubled Pascal, to cite just one example. According to St. John of the Cross, the imagination, instead of fixing itself on the great and lasting truths, goes off "to gather rose-buds" here and there or to lead one astray on a by-path of dreams and idle wishes. So it happens that many build for themselves worlds of fantasy and illusion, castles in Spain wherein they can forget the harsh realities of life.

Even some very devout people fall victim to the weakness of the imagination in an almost ceaseless tendency to forget their own duties, their own calling, and to dream of paths other than the one they should follow. They would like to imitate this or that person whom they know; but they shrink from knowing themselves as they really are. They are quick to imagine how they ought to act in this or that possible difficulty, but they find themselves at a loss in meeting their own daily problems.

This craze for the merely fanciful is not easy to overcome. It troubles a lot of very devoted people and prevents their settling down to their own duties. Thus St. John of the Cross singles out, among those defects which beset those who are seeking perfection in the spiritual life, envy of people more talented or endowed with greater spiritual gifts. And he prudently advises that we should beware of ill-timed wishes to imitate exactly the life of this or that saint because such wishes often lead us to avoid our own plain duty. There is only one life that can always and in all circumstances serve as a model for us. That life is our Lord's, because His is the only life wholly in accord with the truth.

Anything that is not built on Him as the cornerstone will one day crumble; the walls of all those Jerichos so painstakingly assembled by men's dreams will fall to earth before the harsh trumpeting of reality. What we call experience, the bitter readjustment of our lives to reality, thus turns out to be useless for the majority of men except when it is preceded by the clearing away of numerous false ideas. To what purpose is all this waste of life, of experience, of reality? Faith and reason should have permitted men to achieve a much greater result without the necessity of such suffering and such bitter disappointment.

St. Thérèse of Lisieux, though the youngest of novice mistresses, showed herself to be possessed of the soul of a veteran in the way she grounded her spiritual life on the Gospel, following its path of truth from the beginning to the end of her days. Like all the other saints, she teaches that in all temptations and in all the strayings of our imagination, we ought to rely upon our supernatural good sense, always trying to find the eternal and unchanging ways of God in all things. We must strive to dig through the deceptive sand of appearances which conceal everything that is around us, and to find underneath them the rock of reality.

First of all, we must strive to reach our own soul, the only true and lasting reality given directly to us, the permanent source of that fountain of life which we feel surging within us and whose effects we know. It is our primary task to come face to face with our own soul in order to prepare it for everlasting life. Its eternal destiny is directly related to what we do with it here on earth with God's help.

When we are at the very center of this prime reality of our own soul, we find Another Reality. This Reality is Infinite; it is the Reality of God, One in Three Persons. He dwells within the soul and it is there the true contemplative must seek Him. Is He not the most real of all realities? The rock upon which resets and depends everything that is? Is He not the Alpha and Omega, the beginning and the end?

Our faith affirms that from all eternity, we are the chosen objects of the love of this Almighty Being. He wishes us to be His own, and He has of course every means of satisfying His desire to possess us. But with an exquisite degree of divine courtesy, He leaves us free to accept or reject him. Thus He asks of us but one thing—that we offer ourselves, cost what it may, to His reality, so that He may give us freedom. This is all that He asks. He takes upon Himself to do everything else. By means of a wondrous shower of free gifts, He has already established a plan to make us holy. Through His providence He will make the whole world serve our soul. He will order all things and all happenings so that they become ready instruments for the realization of His purposes.

How, then, could we fail to look unceasingly to this Being, who is our Father but who is also our Friend, who is all powerful but also full of love for us?

God and our own soul: to walk in the truth means, fundamentally, to foster the most constant possible awareness of these two deepest realities. "Live in this world as though there were in it but God and thy soul," wrote St John of the Cross,[3] echoing the well-known dictum of St. Teresa: "Be alone with Him only." [4] And Brother Lawrence of the Resurrection said: "After having given myself wholly to God . . . I have trusted that I had nothing else to do for the rest of my days than to live as if there were no one but God and me in the

[3] *Points of Love*, no. 61, 4; Peers III, 232.
[4] *The Life of the Holy Mother Teresa of Jesus*, chap. xxxvi; Peers I, 260.

wished to define what he thought to be the true spirit of Carmel, he used the following formula: "Walk in God's presence, keeping in the state of grace and doing good, while preserving peace of heart within oneself." [1] Such a view was the essential note of St. Teresa's reform as well as a cardinal point of the teaching of St. John of the Cross who instructs us thus in one of this Maxims: "School yourselves always to stay in God's presence."

But how can we do this, or how can we foster the sense of God's presence within us?

It is not so much a matter of making a great effort of mind to realize that presence in our soul, for it is constant and quite independent of us. Our work does not consist in conjuring it up by some kind of artifice. All we need do is simply recognize that God is really there.

This is accomplished in different stages. First we realize that we are encompassed in the divine reality and wholly surrounded by Him. Then we become aware that this great Presence is not limited to the

[1] Père Jerôme de la Mère de Dieu, O.C.D.: *La Doctrine du Venerable Frère Jean de Saint-Samson* (Paris: Editions de la Vie Spirituelle).

mere act of being there. His gaze is constantly upon us. Unfortunately we are unable to respond to this gaze in kind for, face to face with God, we become blinded by the divine reality. We cannot look upon him eye to eye. We must approach Him gradually, making use at first of a thousand efforts which finally merge into one.

Groping about like blind people, it is like them too that we must learn to speak to God, making use of this great means of the sightless to assure themselves of a presence which is not visible to them. Finally, if we are faithful in our practice, we come to a stage when we can "see without seeing," when we have an abiding awareness of God's presence, and when, in the dark glass of faith, God's face is illumined for us.

That is the moment when we realize we are in the presence of the greatest reality of all, or at least that there is no distance separating us from Him.

It is within these innermost depths of the self that each of us must seek to become aware of God. We must discover him there as our Creator, but also as one who is more really ourselves than we are, for in Him "we live and move and have our being" (Acts 17:28).

God is also present in a special way when we live in His grace, as His friends, as His intimates. He "dwells" within our soul and that supernatural relationship is established by which we are His adopted children. As St. John of the Cross reminds us: "the Word, together with the Father and the Holy Spirit, is hidden essentially in the inmost center of the soul. Wherefore, the soul that would find Him through union of love must go forth and hide itself from all created things according to the will and enter within itself in deepest recollection, communing there with God in intimate and affectionate fellowship, esteeming all that is in the world as though it were not. Hence St. Augustine, speaking with God in the *Soliloquies*, said : 'I found thee not, O Lord, without, because I erred in seeking thee without that wert within.' He is, then, hidden within the soul, and there the good contemplative must seek Him." [2]

To find God within the self, we must pierce more and more thoroughly by love into the inner-

[2] *Spiritual Canticle*, Stanza I, 4.

most parts of our soul, as we are taught in *The Living Flame.* "The center of the soul is God. . . . The more degrees of love the soul has, the more profoundly does it enter into God and the more is it centered in Him; and thus we can say that, as are the degrees of love of God, so are the centers, each one deeper than another, which the soul has in God." [3]

The Saint goes on to teach that, even when the soul has attained to the center of its own self, it must not rest content but rather seek ceaselessly to go onward "just as a stone, were it able to bypass all that stands in its way, would fall to the very center of the earth without stopping."

The teaching of St. Teresa does not differ from any of this. She too gives prime importance to the divine indwelling. She too insists on the profound truth of Augustine's words: "In vain did I seek you apart from myself." And it was her practice, as she grew in God's friendship, to think of the divine mysteries as though they were all taking place within her. [4]

While God is thus present within our souls,

[3] *The Living Flame*, Stanza I, n. 12.
[4] Cf. *Life*, chap. IX; Peers I, 56.

37

within their most secret recesses, He is evidently separated from them too; He is as closely united with all other beings as He is with us, for it is to him that everything owes its being and subsistence. "God," says St. John of the Cross, "dwells and is even substantially present in every soul, even in that of the greatest sinner in the world. And this kind of union is ever wrought between God and all the creatures, for in it He is preserving their being: if union of this kind were to fail them, they would at once become annihilated and would cease to be." [5]

We are thus encompassed by God on all sides. In order to express this truth, mystical writers have tried all sorts of daring picturizations, which need not necessarily be to our liking. One is that suggested by Père Chardon when he speaks of a tiny sponge cast into the immensity of the ocean.[6] So is God everlastingly present all about us, even more so than a vast ocean whose tremendous waves we might see thrown up around us, stretching outward toward the horizon. The earth is his and the fulness thereof but it does not suffice to contain Him.

[5] *Ascent of Mount Carmel*, II, 5, 3, Peers I, 75.
[6] Cf. Louis Chardon, O.P.: *The Cross of Jesus*, (St. Louis: B. Herder Book Company, 1959), Chap. V, p. 36.

When the last traces of the upcast spray can no longer be seen, He still remains as He is. Beyond the farthermost limits of all that is material and quantitative, the infinity of pure spirit is just beginning. God is, moreover, everywhere and always present in the world of the angels which, again, his being infinitely surpasses and overflows.

Briefly, God alone can contain Himself. Theologians in their fashion express this by saying that God is present in all things by His power as well as by His nature; for He is present whenever He works in all the fulness of His mysterious life-giving force.

"In the vivid contemplation and knowledge of the creatures, the soul sees with great clearness that there is in them such abundance of graces and virtues and beauty wherewith God endowed them, that (as it seems to her) they are all clothed with marvellous natural beauty, derived from and communicated by that infinite supernatural beauty of the image of God, Whose beholding of them clothes the world and all the heavens with beauty and joy."[7] Thus speaking as a theologian, John of the Cross notes a third mode of God's presence:

[7] *Spiritual Canticle*, Stanza 5, verse 5.

39

God is with all things by the fact that He sees them, that they ever stand in His sight.

God actually sees all things: all things are in His sight. He is not present in the manner of some blind force, some mysterious impulse unconscious of its creative power; but rather as one who sees and who cares, from the depths of His infinite reality.

Surely the realization of this fact should move us and lead us to a more studied comprehension of the divine presence. For if need be we can overlook the presence of someone who is indifferent to us; chance continually places us side by side with those who care nothing at all for us, and whose unseeing glances shift past us without even taking note that we are there. We ourselves ignore these people too.

But when someone gazes upon us insistently, seeking to discover every aspect of our being, we cannot long remain unaware of the fact or indifferent. Even if we do not lift up our own eyes at once, we are (so to speak) magnetized until we return glance for glance.

So when God gazes insistently and constantly upon us, ought we not to acknowledge His glance by at least recognizing His presence—the presence indeed of a supreme reality whose gaze does not stop at the surface of our being but pierces much more deeply, searching the heart and reins. "The Lord beholdeth the heart" (I Kings, 16:7).

He searches within us a thousand times more probingly than any secret rays of the physician can penetrate our inward parts and detect our most hidden functions. God's look, in fact, does not have to probe within us; it is already settled within every part of us, knowing us both outwardly and inwardly, beholding all the fibers of our being, for he is wholly and everywhere present.

We should return again and again in meditation to the expression of St. Paul where he describes for us the qualities of the Word: "living . . . more piercing than any two-edged sword . . . discerner of the thoughts and intents of the heart (Hebrews 4:12). St. Paul insists in fact that no man knows how to hide himself from God. On the contrary, "all things are naked and open to his eyes" (Hebrews 4:13).

It was then vain for Adam and Eve to seek refuge in the hidden places of Eden after they had sinned.

God's eye had never once been turned aside from them and it was only irony that made him ask: "Adam, Where art thou?" In spite of this knowledge, the sinner still clings to the folly of trying to hide himself. He thus deludes himself for, as Scripture tells us, the eyes of the Lord are a thousand times more searching than the sun's rays and He gazes upon every single step of a man (Eccles. 17:13,15).

The word "eyes" are of course used in that text in the metaphorical sense. The Bible boldly employs such language to bring out as clearly as possible the fact that the divine glance searches us ceaselessly and in all its varying manifestations. Varying manifestations indeed: for how reproachfully does God glance upon sinners; how kindly does He view all, good and evil alike, as He showers upon the world the blessings of nature—the sun, and the rain, and the stars; in how graceful a manner does that glance come which fills the souls of the elect with divine life. Once, long ago, there was a special glance filled with all the riches of God's love given to her who is blessed among women and who cried out that "the Lord has regarded the lowliness of His handmaid." God indeed gazes upon us unceasingly with a look that gives life, and the Carmelite saints remind us of this, as when St. John of the Cross puts upon the lips of the soul these words: "Thine eyes imprinted me with thy grace. . . . Now can'st thou indeed look upon me since thou didst look upon me and leave me in grace and beauty."[8]

Such metaphors convey profound truths in symbolic language. Nevertheless, since the Incarnation, it is no longer true to say that God is without real eyes. He took upon himself our flesh; as if He were not content with gazing at us in the spirit as He had theretofore encompassed and searched His creatures, He then began to look upon them with human eyes. St. Mark's Gospel, in speaking of the rich young man, tells us that Jesus, "looking on him, loved him" (10:21). It is thus not only the Father "who sees in secret" (Matt. 6:4,6), who gazes upon us; there is another glance, one that is piercing but also kind, that pursues us as Christ bends lovingly over us from His heavenly abode.

To cultivate in ourselves the knowledge of God's

[8] *Spiritual Canticle*, Stanzas 23, 24.

presence is then to seek to know the face of the Triune God, ever-present, all-powerful, Supreme. But it is also to know our Lord, and not only as He sits at the right hand of the Father but as He abides among us in our tabernacles.

Unfortunately, however, we behave like blind men in the face of such overpowering realities. It is impossible for us to look God in the eye, to return His gaze and fix it upon Him once and for all, remaining united to His brightness without looking away. If we could but once do so, we would remain transfixed in the Beatific Vision without having the least wish to lower our eyes. But on this earth we see His divine reality as in a glass darkly, like a reflection in a mirror.

Such is the doctrine insisted upon by John of the Cross and, for that matter, drawn by him from the most ancient sources: "Aristotle says that even as are the eyes of the bat with regard to the sun, which is total darkness to it, even so is our understanding to that which is greater light in God, which is total darkness to us."[9] God, who is all resplendent

[9] *Ascent*, Book II, chap. VIII, 6; Peers I, 92.

in Himself, casting light throughout the world of the spirit, where He is the true sun of the spirits, as St. Augustine says, is an opaque darkness to our eyes because of His very brightness. He is a star which must be veiled in our saddened world where all spiritual reality, because it is bound up with things of the senses, becomes dimmed. We ourselves, spiritual beings whose bodies are animated by the souls presently within them, are blinded by the very materiality of our bodies. We see only in accordance with material limitations, for everything we know must reach us through the windows of our eyes and our other senses. We cannot bear to look upon the divine gaze. We must be content to walk in the shadows of its light.

"The soul," as the Doctor of Carmel writes, "must rather proceed by not understanding than by desiring to understand; and by blinding itself and setting itself in darkness rather than by opening its eyes, in order the more nearly to approach the ray divine."[10]

We must then act like blind men in order to approach God and to remain in his presence. We must

[10] *Ascent*, II, VIII, 5; Peers, I, 92.

also imitate those continual gropings by which the blind are enabled to find their way; above all, we must speak out and ask for help, as they do, if we are to maintain ourselves in God's presence.

For a beginning we should not disdain even the most humble of means. Methods of course are as varied as are souls themselves. But beginners are sometimes taught to make use of certain aids to memory, i.e., to attach a piece of string to the arm or to the finger so that each time they touch it they will think of God. Aside from these practices, it is good to mark out certain hours of the day by definite signs designed to recall the mind to the thought of God.

Following on such positive means there are also negative ones: doing pennance for frequent forgetfulness of God's presence, i.e., by kneeling down or performing some other slight penitential act. We must not overlook the fact that we are here at the lowest rung, so to speak, of the ladder; nor should we be surprised if we are concerned with what is simply material. As far as these matters are concerned, some more generous souls make use of further means, even doing some kind of penance which, by causing a slight suffering, helps the soul to be reminded of God.

All this striving should result in constant progress. The means should be varied to prevent their becoming ineffective: one always risks the danger of being bound to the letter and forgetting the spirit. Frequent alteration of means is therefore necessary. For just as blind people vary their efforts, always remaining in motion, grasping at walls or at whatever else will help them to get to their objective, so must we display our ingenuity in love, like Mary Magdalen who earnestly sought our Lord everywhere and who finally found Him in the disguise of a gardener. And we, if we be as deeply concerned as she was, will also achieve the object of our search. The soul achieves its end by following its own path to God, constantly striving to remain in His presence and searching to return His glance.

We should also make generous use of prayer. Words, even more than other means, are useful in keeping us in touch with God. Again, speech is the main way by which the blind establish contact with others; just like a glance, a word goes forth in search of the other. It attracts his attention; it compels a response. The laws of conversation are not abandoned in the spiritual order, even if God plays the role of the mute interlocutor.

He sees us but he remains still. We are blind but we speak; He sees but of His own Will chooses to be silent. We would be mistaken were we to refrain from voicing aloud our wishes on the pretext that He already knows what it is we would ask of Him. Our words moreover serve to fix our attention, even if they do not attract His; words help us in this sense to enjoy in a real way the benefits of His presence.

For this reason Carmelite spiritual writers have recommended that we use, at least in the beginning, short prayers or aspirations, clearly articulated. They serve to stave off drowsiness, to keep us from spiritual passivity: for the simple glance of love toward God, however perfect it may be, is not always enough. As Father John of Jesus-Mary wrote: "The soul may be oriented toward God in two ways: either it may confine itself to thinking of Him in the simple way one looks upon a friend, without doing anything more than that; or, better yet, while thinking of Him, the soul may spur itself to love by acts and sentiments in the manner of one who not only looks in amity upon his friend but offers or promises him gifts. . . . The first way may be useful sometimes, as when one wishes to rest the stirrings of the heart by fixing a loving look on Jesus Christ; but generally speaking, this method is not fruitful, nor does it sufficiently rouse the heart. It is therefore better to make more frequent use of the second method."[11]

Prayer of this type requires even greater effort on our part; but this effort more fully impresses our soul and even our body with the habitual recognition of God's presence. The habit of thus speaking spontaneously and unaffectedly to God is much favored among Carmelites because it readily leads us to a form of prayer characteristic of Carmel. This kind of prayer is described by St. Teresa as familiar address to God; and, according to her celebrated definition, mental prayer is no more than frequent solitary conversation with him who we know loves us."[12] This is the usual Carmelite doctrine

[11] Cf. Père Jean de Jésus-Marie: *Instruction des Novices* (Malines: Dessain, 1882), p. 363.
[12] *Life*, Ch. VIII; Peers, I, 50.

and it is constantly encountered in the writings of the Carmelite mystics. John of Saint-Sampson says: "We ought to engage in inward conversation with Him in the spirit, by sweet and familiar speech. Think of what friendly, private conversation is between two friends . . . and then make use of it within the depths of your soul when you are before the divine Majesty."[13] And Brother Lawrence of the Resurrection writes: "we ought to form a habit of thinking of the presence of God by conversing with Him continually, for it is a shameful thing to abandon conversation with Him to consider trifles."[14] So general is the practice of conversing with God that a wonderful anthology might be made of the invocations which the Carmelite saints have addressed to Him to keep alive in their souls a sense of His presence.

These aspirations, or short prayers, are like the incessant efforts of the blind man who fears that somehow God may have left him. As the hart pants, so does he; and he wishes constantly to prolong his conversation with God. He is like a lover

[13] *Opera Omnia* I, p. 306.
[14] *Practice of the Presence of God, op. cit.,* p. 64.

who is constantly saying: "Are you still with me? Are you still my Beloved?"

In due time everything becomes more simple. Just as a blind man acquires by force of habit a special sense of touch, so the soul which faithfully strives to recollect itself finds the means of doing this more and more easy. It is not always aware of this progress, for this is something that transpires in obscurity. It does not burst forth all at once in that canticle of liberation which St. John of the Cross would have it sing: "I went forth from myself— that is, from my low manner of understanding, from my weak way of loving, and from my poor and limited manner of experiencing God."[15]

Before this simplification comes about, however, the soul must endure some moments when the thought of God is extremely painful rather than easy or consoling. Efforts must now be made in a different direction: instead of cultivating the sense of God's presence, the soul is now oppressed with doleful memories and laments his absence. In these periods of anxiety, the soul fears that it is not suf-

[15] *The Dark Night of the Soul* II, 4, 1; Peers, I, p. 380.

ficiently devoted to God and is disturbed by such thoughts.

In point of fact these occasions are good for the soul. They mark its progress toward a realization of God's presence which is more and more spiritual, less and less tainted with selfishness and things of that sort. St. John of the Cross himself tells us that this anguish is a sign that we are entering on the contemplative path, that our course is set in the right direction.[16] If, then, the soul continues to be faithful, the time will surely and quickly come when it is no longer en route, according to the admirable expression of St. John.

It has now risen above mere methods; it can apply to itself what Brother Lawrence of the Resurrection has ingenuously said of his own arrival at the summit of the spiritual life: "People seek for methods of learning to love God. They hope to arrive at it by I know not how many different practices; they take much trouble to remain in the presence of God in a quantity of ways. Is it not much shorter and more direct to do everything for the love of God, to make use of all the labors of

[16] *Ascent*, II, 4, passim

one's state in life to show Him that, and to maintain
His presence within us by the communion of our
hearts with His? There is no finesse about it; one
has only to do it generously and simply."[17] There is
of course a great simplification here. But by this
doctrine the soul could ever be with God, just as
Brother Lawrence was. We are told by his first
biographer that "he found God everywhere, as
much while he was repairing shoes as while he was
praying with the community. He was in no hurry
to make his retreats because he found in his ordinary work the same God to love and to adore as in
the depths of the desert." [18]

Henceforth the soul finds less need to speak to
the Lord: words are now become a burden. The
soul will no doubt still direct many cries to heaven;
it will express many thoughts of love destined to
reach God's heart. But these prayers of aspiration
have become so simple that they scarcely find expression on the lips. Words would be too heavy
for them; they would impede the flights of love.
The soul thus puts completely into practice what

[17] *Practice of the Presence of God, op. cit.*, p. 49
[18] *Ibid.* p. 53

John of Saint-Sampson calls "aspiration," a kind of exercise he commends to souls already purified and one which unites them to God in a bond that is wholly spiritual. "It is," he writes, "an ardent impulsion of the heart and soul, warm in love, by which the soul transcends itself and all created things, in order that it may move into closer union with God."[19] The soul is no longer limited to painful clutching at a presence; now it literally runs to its Final End and Object as naturally as a river seeks the sea, or a rock falls to the ground.

In this way the creature returns by love to the God who in love called it forth from Himself when he gave it being. It flows back to its Source and is absorbed in It. And thus the miracle is accomplished toward which the soul has directed all its generous efforts, for which it has received many aids, in pursuit of which it has engaged in the slow and painful travail of grace. Without doubt God is still seen in the light of faith, for no man may gaze directly on the face of God; but already tender love is king of night. As the Psalmist tells us, night shall be light as day as the eyes of the Lord shine upon his servant (Ps. 138:12; Ps. 40:16). No longer

[19] Cf. *La Doctrine du Vénérable Frère Jean de Saint-Samson, op. cit.,* p. 34.

is night clad in its dark and heavy mantle; this is "the night now near to the light of day"[20] in which the shape of things begins to be bathed in an ineffably beautiful light; or so at least it seems to the soul when, in the dark obscurity of faith, it confronts the glance of God.

The soul never thought it had more than faith to offer it a real picture of Him Whom it sought; but now the soul moves forward to enter into a personal experience of things hoped for. Faith grants it an experience of "those eyes desired,"[21] those eyes which have mirrored the invisible glance as the soul gazed upon its love, just as one can see mirrored in a clear spring the face of one who bends over it. But now the soul sees what is unseen; now, as the mystics are so fond of saying, it "sees without seeing." For it has cleansed its inner eye in purity; and, though still blinded, it now gazes upon God and lives in the spirit before Him. It has founded its spiritual life upon the rock; and as Teresa of Avila wished, "it goes forth in truth," illumined by the light of God's searching glance.

[20] *Ascent*, I, 2, 5; *Spiritual Canticle* (A), Stanza 14, n. 23; Peers I, 20.
[21] *Spiritual Canticle* Stanza XI, 4.

3

Presence To Oneself

CARMELITE spiritual writers seem to have a
special mission to recall to our minds one of
the most profound, meaningful verses of the Gospel: "The Kingdom of God is within you" (Luke
17:21). Their teaching is an unceasing reminder
of the *interior* life. St. Teresa, in speaking of the
soul, describes it as a wonderful castle and she urges
us to be unsatisfied with remaining in the moats or
even in the outer chambers only but to penetrate
to the very heart of the castle where God resides.

Admittedly, we have a great need of being stimu-
lated through such language to undertake this
search within ourselves. Are we not among those
souls whom the Saint has described as "so infirm

and so accustomed to busying themselves with out-side affairs that nothing can be done for them, and it seems as though they are incapable of entering within themselves at all."[1] We lead our lives as though we were "buried in externals," as the *Imitation* puts it (Bk. I, c. XXI, 4); we are mainly pre-occupied with what shows, not with what is true. If our thoughts turn to others, it is less to give them the best of ourselves than to satisfy our own curiosity about them, and often to judge them un-justly. Even reflection on ourselves and our acts is frequently motivated by the desire to play some kind of heroic role in our own eyes, or in the impression we make on others.

In place of such unworthy thoughts, the admirable doctrine of the Carmelite writers proposes that we try to plumb the depths of our own souls to try to understand them as they are. Is not our own soul the one great reality with which we come into contact through knowledge gained within ourselves? And is not our own soul the main path toward knowledge and love of God?

[1] St. Teresa, *Interior Castle*, First Mansions, c. I; Peers II, 203

The soul is profoundly worthy of our consideration and study. The Carmelite tradition bids us
reflect upon its greatness, even in the merely natural
sense. St. Teresa heard our Lord say to her: "It
(thy soul) is not lowly, daughter, for it is made in
My Image."[2] On her own part, the Saint declares:
"I can find nothing with which to compare the
great beauty of a soul and its great capacity. In fact,
no matter how acute our intellects may be, they will
no more be able to attain to a comprehension of this
than to an understanding of God; for as He Himself says, He created us in His Image and Likeness."[3]
Therefore, "in speaking of the soul we must always
think of it as spacious, ample, and lofty; and this
can be done without the least exaggeration, for the
soul's capacity is much greater than we can realize."[4]
What wonderful words these are, and how splendid
are the horizons they open to us!

Yet St. John of the Cross surpasses even these
words by saying: "One single thought of a man is
of greater worth than the whole world."[5]

[2] *Spiritual Relations*, n. LIV; Peers, I, 361.
[3] *Interior Castle*, First Mansions, c. 1; Peers, II, 201
[4] *Ibid.*, c. II; Peers, II, 208.
[5] Spiritual Sentences and Maxims, n. 32; Peers III, 222.

Knowledge of the self, the necessity for which is thus set forth by the Carmelite mystics, has a high and noble aim: namely, to put us in touch with the great reality called the soul, to make us discover our own souls. This is indeed knowledge of a very sublime order. As John of Saint-Sampson says: "To know oneself is the greatest knowledge of all. It is more valuable to know the beauty of one's own soul than to know how excellent are the angels, how wide the heavens, how fruitful and fecund the earth and the seas. . . . All these are outside of us, but the soul is within."[6]

There is a vast difference between a feverish, never-satisfied book-knowledge, and that simple but noble understanding attained by those who have learned how to live with the soul that is within them. Clearly, one does not arrive at this kind of self-knowledge all at once. It requires a studied effort, and one that will always be at a handicap. Were we angels, we would have a light-giving and intuitive knowledge of our own essential nature and would thus see at a glance each aspect of ourselves as well as the whole. Our soul, however,

[6] *Opera*, I, p. 525

exists within the limitations of the flesh; and just as these limitations constitute a barrier between us and God, causing his light to be a kind of darkness to us, so do they prevent our seeing ourselves. We must then set out in pursuit of ourselves, searching for ourselves incessantly so that we may know ourselves, striving to gain from the observance of our own acts an awareness of our natural leanings: for it is by its fruit that a tree is known and judged.

But what practical method can we follow to know ourselves, as we must to attain a knowledge of God?

It is called the Examination of Conscience, and is a means which will go hand in hand with a sense of God's presence. If faithfully followed, it will engender in us an habitually pure intention which will truly allow us to live and to walk in the way of truth.

Examination of Conscience

The examination of conscience ought to have a fixed place in our daily schedule: so fixed indeed within the framework of our daily rounds that it would be impossible to set it aside or to dispense with it in any way.

There are two principal times when, according to the Carmelite or almost any other rule, this exercise is explicitly provided for. A little before midday "all will meet in choir or in another place of prayer and there they shall examine their consciences for about ten minutes." In one form or another, the various religious orders have always made use of this sort of self-examination around lunch-time, affording their members an opportunity to check up on themselves, to take account briefly of their state of soul. For the soul that really wishes to pursue spiritual perfection, this practice is a precious invitation to benefit from the wisdom of the church. The middle of the day is the hour of special temptation, of that noon-day devil of whom the Psalmist speaks (90:6); a time given over to satisfying our material needs that sting the body sharply, that demand sustenance for it, even at the price of invading the body with sluggishness. The soul which began its day in newness and joy in the morning hours now senses itself to be a prey to lassitude; it must make concessions to the body so that bodily strength may be renewed. For these reasons noon is a perfect time for the soul to draw up a kind of balance sheet of what it has been doing, to render an account of its works in the space of a few minutes before this excellent opportunity is gone.

At night it is necessary to examine onself again, casting a glance over the whole day that has just past. Before the night comes on in which, as our Lord told us, "no man can work" (John 9:4), we try to hold the entire day within our hands, so to speak, before it vanishes forever. That is the moment when we ought to try to draw down a blessing on the day that is over, by offering that day to God and admitting all our faults and failings to his loving heart so that he may wipe them away and put them out of memory, thus assuring us that this day will not later be a burden to draw us backward. The Carmelite Constitutions recommend that this examination be made before the final night prayers; and all Carmelite mystics look upon it as something indispensable.

The use of the examination of conscience is also recommended for other times during the day, as for example on every occasion when we turn to God in prayer. One spiritual writer suggests that we ought to prepare for prayer by setting before ourselves three questions: "Who is this God to whom I desire to offer my petition? Who am I to ask it of Him? What is it that I desire in my prayer?" Although the form of these questions may seem rather artificial, it is certainly possible for us to linger on the second point, the practical consequences of which would be to begin one's prayer with a short examination of conscience and perhaps a *Confiteor*. St. Teresa taught nothing less to her subjects: "To pray as we ought . . . the first things must be examination of conscience, confession of sin, and the signing of yourself with the Cross."[7]

How is our examen, as it is called, to be made? Let us see first of all what it should not be.

The examen is not a matter that requires us to take stock of things with an implacable exactitude. Its aim is to reveal to us our soul, and this cannot be achieved by concentrating on material affairs, numbers, etc. If we try to bring before our eyes every

[7] *Way of Perfection*, c. xxvi; Peers, II, 106.

single imperfection of which we have been guilty, we shall generally be wasting our time. It is true that certain spiritual writers of Carmel seem to stress minutiae. Father John of Jesus-Mary, for example, writes: "Examine in a brief and orderly fashion each one of your acts since your last examen. To what end and in what way have you conducted yourself? What duties have you left undone? What inspirations to virtue have you neglected? How many good inspirations have you rejected and what were they? How many words have you spoken? how many heard?"[8] We ought not to follow this method literally, for the writer wished rather to place before young novices of the Carmelite Order an example of a most complete examen than to give them a plan which they were to follow *in toto* each time. For that matter, he elsewhere shows himself to be much more concise and presents us with a scheme which we would do well to remember: "One should usually survey oneself under three heads, such as thought, words and actions, calling to mind what one recollects of each without dwelling upon unnecessary details. To these we should

[8] *Vade-Mecum*, p. 71.

add another important head, the matter of omissions."

The more the soul advances, the more it feels the need to simplify this exercise; and it is gratifying to note that the greater mystics generally give the more broad-minded advice. St. Teresa, for example, describes the knowledge of self as being one of the mansions of the Interior Castle; the soul enters within it by means of the examination of conscience; the Saint insists, however, that in this chamber, we must "move about freely". For her, liberty is indeed a basic principle of the whole life of devotion: "No soul which practices prayer . . . should be subjected to undue constraint or limitation. Since God has given it such dignity it must be allowed to roam through these mansions—through those above, those below, and those on either side. It must not be compelled to remain for a long time in one single room—not, at least, unless it is the room of self-knowledge."[9]

How broad-minded is the Saint to take this large view of things! And we may draw a lesson from these words regarding the freedom with which

[9] *Ibid.* Peers II, 208.

the soul ought to make its examen, realizing that it should not become too fastly bound to any one method that would narrow the soul or cause it to get caught up completely in self-knowledge. As St. Teresa charmingly writes of this latter danger: the soul would "thus cling so closely to its own hive that it would never go forth as it should, in imitation of the bee who gathers honey from more than one flower."[10] Let this lesson of freedom as taught by the great Saint bear fruit, then, in our own lives. By simplifying the examen as much as we can, we are able to reduce its exercise to just the principal headings of self-examination.

The essential thing is to look at oneself objectively, as though we were being judged by another. As St. Bernard said: "Set yourself before your own face as if it were the face of another." St. Anthony wished his disciples to write down their faults as though they were under an obligation to render account of themselves to someone.

This of course is no easy matter. One will never achieve it in the first attempt, for we must first of all suppress the urge to self-justification which is

[10] *Ibid*, Peers, II, *Ibid*.

so deeply rooted in our nature since the Fall. Both
Adam and Eve excused themselves to God, each
one saying "It was not my fault." And the child,
who is after all a man not yet grown up, instinc-
tively says "It was not I who did it." Our Lord, in
the Parable of the Pharisee and the Publican, has
described this repulsive streak in our nature: the
Pharisee would not have been displeasing to God
had he merely recalled the good he had done; but
his prayer was inacceptable because he tried to veil
his faults by hiding them under his good deeds. The
Publican on the other hand confessed to God his
own unworthiness because he was forcing himself
to be true to himself. He is the one we must take as
our model as we look upon ourselves as "the ac-
cused" before God's tribunal, without trying to
make excuses to God so that we may avoid putting
ourselves in the position of one who undertakes his
own defense.

The resolution to respect the truth is therefore
essential so that it may have a total effect on the
whole body of those imperfections which searching
memory allows us to uncover; or so that it may
focus attention on one or two of our evident fail-

ings as we have noted them; or, as will happen more frequently, so that it may rest upon the whole obscure complexus of those imperfections we daily nourish, that "flock we lead to pasture" so carefully, as St. John of the Cross calls them.[11]

In this light, we will truly accuse ourselves of all that comes to mind, thus proving ourselves to be possessed of that liberty which St. Teresa tells us is ours in the midst of self-knowledge, all the while taking account of our dispositions for the day when, "gathering up our imperfections," we may fashion them into the honey of compunction.

In this way we will learn to know our own soul. To say it once more, the soul does not readily yield itself to the exactions of a rigid formalism. But it can be fathomed and scanned by one who is determined to make use of every means to see things as they really are.

In addition to our fundamental loyalty to the truth, there is a second principle of self-examination which is essential. St. John of the Cross expresses it thus: "Without thee, Lord, naught will be

[11] Cf. *Spiritual Canticle* (A) stanza 19, n. 5.

accomplished."[12] Our own earnest efforts to be truthful in the study of ourselves will not amount to much if it does not prepare us to receive another light—the only light which will allow us to see clearly, the light infused by God. As John of Jesus-Mary taught his disciples: "Seek the light of divine grace in order to see your many faults."[13] It is thus necessary that a notable part of our examen should be devoted to asking light of God; for then, as a ray of sunshine which strikes a dark place reveals all the dust of the air as it turns and dances in its brightness, so does God's light show us to ourselves as we are.

Close contact with God is necessary for man to see his sinfulness. "Depart from me, O Lord, for I am a sinful man," exclaimed St. Peter, when Christ had miraculously shown himself to him on the Lake. And Zacchaeus, when the Lord was passing by him on the street, seemed to have been awakened from a long sleep and to have come to a knowledge of his sinful state. He later exclaimed "If I have wronged any man of anything, I restore him four-

[12] *Spiritual Sentences and Maxims*, prol.; Peers, III, 218.
[13] *Vade-Mecum*, c. LV, par. 15, no. 3.

fold" (Luke 19:8). The centurion was at first willing that Jesus come to him to cure his servant but, as the Master drew near, he became so aware of his own failings that he sent out his friends to tell him: "Lord, I am not worthy that you should enter under my roof . . . just say the word, and my servant shall be healed" (Luke 7:6).

In our examen, God's light will cause us to see our faults as they are; it will be God who will show us our wretched state. So great is the grace of truth that this will be more than the knowledge of reason alone; we will *see* our wretchedness, taste it and savor it. The contemplatives and the saints, abased in their humility to a point we sometimes think excessive, saw things truly; and they were right. The divine rays fell across their souls and lit up before them their most secret places; like animals surprised in their lairs, all those weaknesses to which our human infirmity is always prepared to adjust itself were revealed, and eventually overcome.

John of Saint-Sampson, following St. Bernard, stressed the difference between what he called *reasoned humility*, the fruit of the reasoning faculties, and *impassioned humility*, which is born of God's infused light. The first of these "is controlled by a fully persuaded and convinced reason, but it is not lasting; it is as impermanent as plaster ornamentation, and there is no chance at all for it to outlast a direct divine influence. For if there be more of reason than of love to guide our humility, it is nothing other than a feigned and showy virtue that cannot withstand battle. On this account humility should be the child of love rather than of reason."

Then there is impassioned humility. "Here reason gives way and man is rapt in eternal silence; something is achieved beyond his mental powers, his reason, and indeed his very self: he sees in the light of God's bright light how all human power if the plaything of a day."[14]

The third ingredient of a good examination of conscience is its concern for the future. A firm purpose of not sinning again is of special significance. In the eyes of John of Jesus-Mary, it is of basic and essential importance: "The essential note of this entire matter is the firmness of our resolution

[14] *La Doctrine du V. F. Jean du Saint-Samson*, p. 88-89.

to amend."[15] Those hours then are sterile and profit-lessly wasted in which the soul simply reflects on its misdeeds and errors.

Assuredly we should regret our faults, but we should also do so in a peaceful way. As Brother Lawrence of the Resurrection winningly tells us: "When I realize that I have sinned, I agree and say 'This is my nature, it is what I usually do.' "[16]

These are feelings which touch God's heart. They are feelings too which correspond wonder-fully to the spirit characteristic of Carmel—a spirit which bids us enlarge our confidence in God, to place but small reliance upon ourselves, even to be glad to our own wretchedness. Let us recall the joy with which St. Thérèse of the Child Jesus un-covered her imperfections just a short time before her death, and we will not be discouraged in any way by the sight of our faults but rather filled with hope for the future. And in this connection let us always remember the encouraging words our Lord loved to lavish on the sick whom he had cured: "Go and sin no more" (John 8:11).

[15] *Vade-Mecum*, p. 71
[16] *Practice of the Presence of God*, p. 73.

Purity of Intention

Fidelity, especially willing fidelity, to the examination of conscience eventually fosters within the soul the habit of seeing itself clearly. There naturally follows from this a greater practical realization of God's presence and indwelling in us—something which likewise owes its growth to more or less painful and repeated efforts and which finally develops into an almost continual awareness. Thus, as a result of many sincere examens, the soul acquires the habit of seeing itself as it is. What has up to then been so costly for it has now turned into a source of assurance and of peace. For doesn't habit engender in the soul a certain facility as well as a cheerful inclination to repeat the acts which formed the habit?

From this point of view, certain Carmelite writings which would otherwise seem somewhat surprising become altogether comprehensible.

One of these is the counsel given by St. Teresa: "In all you do and at all times, examine your conscience."[17] Is not this too much to ask of the soul,

[17] *Maxims*, n. 27; Peers III, 257.

especially on the part of one who would have the soul so free in the midst of its self-knowledge? A similar instruction seems to be contained in the first of the twenty rules of perfection given by Christ to St. Maria Magdelena de' Pazzi: "I expect from you that in your every action, internal and external, you have your eyes fixed on that purity that I made known to you. All the works that you will do, all the words that you will say, you must consider as your last."[18] It is clear that these texts do not enjoin an "exercise" properly so called, as if to compel one to precede and to accompany every action by a methodical and systematic examen. This would not only be discouraging, but would lead to useless self-analysis.

What is in question is rather an habitual attitude that is acquired by seeing oneself as one is, a kind of habit which results in an effortless awareness of any imperfections we may have. This habit is called "purity of intention."

[18] *Seraph Among Angels: The Life of St. Mary Magdalene de' Pazzi Carmelite and Mystic*, By Sister Mary Minima, Carmelite, translated from the Italian and edited by the V. Rev. Gabriel N. Pausback, O. Carm. (Chicago: The Carmelite Press, 1958) p. 125.

Thanks to its many efforts, the soul has now become complete master of itself. It can sing with the Psalmist those beautiful words which so moved Sister Elizabeth of the Trinity: " 'My soul is continually in my hands' And what can this mean except perfect self-control in the presence of the Peaceful?"[19] This self-possession is rooted in those things the soul has learned about avoiding self-deceit and gaining self-knowledge. It now knows itself so thoroughly that it cannot escape its own grip "even for the time it would take to say the Creed"[20] It no longer looks about for distractions or even desires them; for it knows, as another beautiful expression of St. John of the Cross has it, that "he who loses an opportunity to pray is like one that has let a bird fly out of the hand; for he will not regain it."[21]

Of course when the soul is so self-possessed, it

[19] *The Spiritual Doctrine of Sister Elizabeth of the Trinity*, by M. M. Philipon, O. P. (Westminster, Md.: The Newman Press, 1961. First Retreat Second day, p. 223.
Sister Elizabeth (1880-1906), a Discalced Carmelite, died a saintly death at the Carmel of Dijon.

[20] St. John of the Cross, *Points of Love*, 61, 6; Peers, III, 233.

[21] *Spiritual Sentences and Maxims*, n. 29; Peers III, 222.

immediately perceives the slightest variations without the need of any lengthy examination. This all takes place quickly and easily; and in the same fashion the soul asks God's pardon and is absolved of its failings.

Purity of intention is not only due to the soul's self-mastery, however, but also, and above all, because it is overwhelmed by God's infused light and in this light sees all its imperfections. The inward eye has become as clear-sighted as our Lord wishes it to be; it lights up the whole field of self-consciousness, and before its piercing brightness the slightest faults stand out. They are perceived at once. "If we consider a ray of sunlight entering through a window, we see that the more the ray is charged with atoms and particles of matter, the more palpable, visible and bright it appears to the eye of sense."[22]

Such purity of intention makes the soul pleasing in God's eyes. Hence St. John of the Cross makes the following homely comparison: "Hair that is combed with frequency is untangled, and there will be no difficulty in combing it as often as one de-

[22] St. John of the Cross, *Ascent*, II, XIV, 9; Peers, I, 115.

sires; and the soul that frequently examines its thoughts, words and deeds, which are like the hair, and that does all things for love of God, will find that its hair is quite free from entanglement. Then the Spouse will look upon the neck of the Bride, and will be captivated thereby, and will be wounded by one of her eyes, namely by the purity of intention wherewith she performs all her acts."[23]

The Carmelite mystics do not confine themselves to the mere description of this exquisite purity of conscience. They give us numerous examples of it in their lives. The story is well-known of the scruple which troubled St. John of the Cross one evening when, being ill, he had asked to have his food before the others in the community, and how he punished himself for this forgetfulness of the rule. During his entire life, he had faithfully observed every aspect of the rule, though he was never indiscreet or excessive in his zeal.

And there are some delightful tales told of his final days, many of them within belief. According to one, St. John was on his way to Ubeda where he eventually died, and worn out with fatigue, he sat

[23] *Points of Love*, n. 26; Peers, III, 228-9.

down by a river to rest. Though it was not the season for asparagus, he began to wish that he could have some for his supper when, as if by miracle, his companion discovered a bunch of the longed-for delicacy on the bridge. John, moved partly by humility and partly (one would suppose) by scrupulosity, as though the asparagus were not rightfully his, asked that half the bunch be left on a nearby rock "for the poor man who had gathered it."

Another time, as he lay on his death-bed at Ubeda, he was asked if he would like to hear some musicians who were in the neighborhood and who wished to comfort him with their playing. At first the Saint agreed to the proposal, but then changed his mind, telling the brother who was nursing him: "Brother, I am very grateful to you for your kindness in my regard, and I appreciate it very much; but since God has granted me the great pains from which I suffer, why should they be sweetened and lessened by music? Thank, therefore, these gentlemen, for the kindness they wish to show me. I regard it as having been done. Recompense them, and send them away."

These may be small matters, but they tell us

79

much about a purity of conscience which the most lengthy examination would not insure. It is rather the work of God's own hand.

Brother Lawrence of the Resurrection had a similar clarity of vision, as when he avowed "that he had attained to having no thoughts except of God; and when he wished to remove some other thought or temptation that he felt coming . . . when exterior occupations diverted him a little from the thoughts of God, there came to him from the Lord some remembrance which took possession of his soul, giving him some most engrossing ideas of God."[24]

Another Carmelite Saint, this time one closer to our own age, Thérèse of the Child Jesus, deprived herself out of fidelity to grace of some little pleasures she had with a pocket knife; according to her rule, she was not entitled to keep this within her cell at night and she therefore faithfully laid it outside the door of her cell.

This exquisite purity of judgment, which is at once the fruit of the soul's own generous effort and

[24] *The Practice of the Presence of God*, pp 74, 75.

of the light given by God, is a reward to souls who have learned to see themselves as they are.

In all these matters, the fundamental question is that of practical truth. This is what is sought after before all else in Carmelite spirituality, for on it is established the whole order of the interior life and inner truthfulness.

To set off in search of this truth means that one must accustom oneself to detachment from all petty falsehoods and dissimulations, to whatever degree they are conscious. Some of them are even present in devout souls. We can realize at what price such detachment is achieved by re-reading the description given by St. John of the Cross of defects and faults in those whom he styles "beginners" and in whom the seven deadly sins show themselves under a pious guise.[25] They are also present in those souls who, without yet being finally established in the truth, believe themselves to be good. Only by seeing their faults through God's eyes can they be led, little by little, to realize that they are no more than unprofitable servants, as our Lord calls them

[25] *Dark Night*, I, chaps 2-7; Peers I, 19-39.

in the Gospel, or to speak with greater exactitude, of no account whatsoever.

If anyone should imagine this last statement an exaggeration, let him consider those scriptural passages which tell of man's wretched state; or listen to the words uttered by even the prophets as they realized, both in the depths of their own hearts as well as in the knowledge of God, that they were themselves nothing. Abraham, at the time he prayed God to have pity on the people of Sodom, said: "Seeing I have begun, I will speak to my Lord, whereas I am dust and ashes" (Gen. 18:27). Moses on his part discovered that he did not know how to speak at all (Exodus 6:30). And it was the same with Jeremias who exclaimed: "Ah! Ah! Lord God: behold, I cannot speak, for I am a child" (Jeremias 1:6). And there are many other similar avowals spoken by the prophets in those fleeting moments when they were in touch with eternal truth.

We can consider ourselves truthful, we will be set free by the truth, only when we know how to see ourselves as we really are in absolute sincerity. Meditating on our faults and weaknesses in this fashion, we will sense and touch those profound wants which are at the root of our wretchedness. There is not only the wretchedness that arises from original sin and from all our personal sins but also from that state of creaturehood which makes us aware, like Israel's prophets, of our own nothingness. It is precisely this which, in the final analysis, makes us "dust and ashes" in God's sight. The consciousness of such profound humility is, we should note, a primary object of Carmelite teaching.

To be in the truth means to walk in the truth as well: God's light is all-pervasive. Thus there is a conflict of light and darkness taking place in every soul: such is the epic conflict described by St. John at the beginning of his Gospel. In this battle more and more do we know ourselves to be sinners of ourselves, and that we shall grow all the more as we abase ourselves in the consciousness of our nothingness. In this respect there is a situation that parallels that of which we have already spoken, in dealing with the presence of God at the soul's center.

Perhaps the word "parallel" is not precise; actually it is the same thing. For the soul, piercing center after center in its search for God, sinks down further into its own humility, probes its wretchedness, and plunges into its very depths, "hiding itself in its own nothingness," as St. John very well puts it.[26] "For upon this road, to go down is to go up; and to go up, to go down, for he that humbles himself is exalted, and he that exalts himself is humbled."[27]

In proportion as the soul abandons himself to Him, God slowly penetrates within it, wisely causing his strength to become a part of it. He does not wish to have his own glory confounded with that of men: "I the Lord, that is my name; I will not give my glory to another" (Isaias 42:8).

How could he tolerate any compromise between his own pure glory and that of men, whose glory is only transient like the flowers of the grass that wither? Thus the wise soul will comport itself with that deep humility which will incline God to redouble his care; for God cannot resist the humble. He loses his heart to them, for they have found

[26] *Other Maxims*, n. 5; Peers, III, 235.
[27] *Dark Night*, II, XVIII, 2; Peers, I, 433.

the path which leads to that heart. A re-reading of the Gospel ought to convince us of this: the Canaanite woman was worthy of being heard because she acknowledged her own unworthiness. "Yes, Lord, but even the dogs eat of the crumbs that fall from their masters' table" (Matthew 15:27). If, then, we wish to walk in the path of truth and to make progress in it, let us not try to justify ourselves in the Lord's eyes nor to hide our faults from him. On the contrary, we should openly show him our weaknesses, avowing them to be what they are as we continually exclaim: "Yes, Lord, but. . . ." Even as we fall, let us call upon heaven, sending a plea to God which will lift us up to him. This is the secret of those who are perfect; this is the way they make constant progress.

Brother Lawrence of the Resurrection seems to have known very well this custom of prayerful souls, this difficult art of "making use of one's faults" so that God's help is unceasingly implored. His biographer tells us that "he always appealed to God when he was proposing to himself the practice of some virtue, saying to him: 'My God, I would not be able to do that if thou didst not help me' and that immediately he was given enough strength and more."[28]

[28] *Practice of the Presence of God, op. cit.,* p. 68.

In such an endeavor the soul will find its purity. It will find too that likeness to God which was its own by creation.

There is a very beautiful dialogue by St. Mary Magdalene de' Pazzi on the subject of the divine purity and its indwelling within us. It depicts that high yearning of prayerful souls who, as a result of fidelity in their attention to their examen, have gradually learned to see themselves as they really are and have acquired that precious self-knowledge whose importance outweighs all other. Seeing themselves, knowing themselves to be wretched and poor, they pant like the hart after the fountain of water, desiring to plunge, to immerse themselves in the immense and infinite purity of God, until they finally lose themselves in him.

Here is the dialogue:

The soul: Tell me, O Father, I pray you, what is this purity? I do not understand it.
The Father: It is an inward cleanness of the heart

which causes the soul to direct all its works to me as well as all its purposes, thus assuring to it everlasting innocense.

The Soul: Is this purity very pleasing to you?

The Father: Understand me well: it indeed pleases me greatly, almost more than I please myself . . . I will say more: So greatly am I pleased to see in a soul a burning desire to share in my purity that, were it possible or fitting that I could so abase myself I would pray that soul to ask it of me and to dispose itself well to receive it, although the very act of daring to wish it and to ask for it be in some sense an offense. . . . In order to acquire this purity, your memory must be fixed, your understanding absorbed, your will annihilated, your heart bemused by love and yet still more awake than ever to hear all that I desire you to know. So much is to be said of the means of gaining this purity, insofar as a creature is capable of doing so. . . . Whosoever would attain to my purity must rise above all created things in heaven and on earth. . . . Such a soul must be devoted to me alone, to my everlasting Reality, counting every thought and every tie (no matter what its nature) as nothing; for the least attachment to created things will be an obstacle to gaining this purity, or will stain it, should one have already attained it."[29]

[29] St. Maria Magdelena de' Pazzi, *Oeuvres*, t. 1, pp 228-243.

4

The Encounter with God
in Prayer

THROUGH realization of God's presence and the faithful practice of the examination of conscience, the soul has put before itself the two great realities which matter most to it: God and itself. From the very beginning there is one certain way of establishing an encounter between these two realities, a path on which the soul can meet its God. That path is prayer.

Two principles seem to govern the Carmelite conception of prayer. First of all, love prevails over reason or methodical discourse. Secondly, the living and delectable encounter with God comes about as the desired, longed-for consequence of the utmost extension of human means. There is, then, a loving search for God; and for generous souls, this search most frequently issues in an encounter that is delectable to the soul. In the course of our discussion, we shall see in what sense the term "delectable" is to be understood.

The Search For God

We should begin by strongly affirming the primacy of love, which is the very root of all attempts to search for God. Love is the beginning; for if we are truly to go in search of our Lord, must we not go outside ourselves? As St. Teresa wrote: "When the presence of God is not felt, we must seek it . . . just as the Bride sought it in the *Canticle*."[1] It is, indeed, in the actual steps of that Bride that we must walk: "I will rise, and will go about the city: in the streets and broad ways I will seek him whom my soul loveth" (Canticle of Canticles, 3:2).

It is love alone that can spur the soul to this

[1] *Interior Castle*, Sixth Mansions, chap, VII; Peers II, 306.

quest without which there could be no encounter at all with God. Of its very nature it is "ecstatic"; the mystics, and especially John of Saint-Sampson, recall this to us, for since thought remains focused on itself, it runs the risk of shutting up within itself the realities which it seeks to possess. We can therefore assert that those who are partisans of intellectualism in prayer are often willing prisoners of methods, and find it very difficult to go out from themselves. St. John of the Cross, on the contrary, describes the "going out of one's house" (that is to say, of oneself) as entirely natural to the soul "kindled in love," and within whose heart there "flames that love which also guides."[2] St. Teresa has also explained this very clearly: "The soul's profit . . . consists not in thinking much but in loving much."[3] She even goes so far as to berate the intelligence "which is merely making itself a nuisance."[4] And John of Saint-Sampson goes her one better by speaking of it as a mere hunting dog; for, as he says, "The understanding, having pic-

[2] *Ascent* I, 1; *Dark Night* I, 1; Peers I, pp. 17, 329
[3] *Foundations*, c. V; Peers III, 20.
[4] *Life*, c. XV; Peers I, 91.

tured the work of God, having seen and sufficiently grasped their meaning, ought to give them to the will that it may be incited and spurred onward. It is the same as with a hunting dog: one makes use of him and allows him to take his prey; but one does not permit him to feast on it. The understanding likewise is not to be permitted to dwell more than is fitting upon the light and truth it has discovered."[5] On his part, Lawrence of the Resurrection is brief: "In the way of God, thoughts count for little; love does everything."[6]

All this testimony, and there is more besides, proves that love has primacy in the Carmelite notion of prayer. It is love alone which permits the soul to rise up above itself to search for God and to encounter him.

Prayer, then, is the path, and the only one, to God. To this point St. Teresa ever returns in her writings. Speaking to those "who wish to travel on this road," she encourages their advance along the path in these words: "There is no other way for those who would reach the fountain of divine life

[5] *La Doctrine* . . . , p. 138
[6] *Practice of the Presence of God, op. cit.*, p. 49.

springing forth from contemplative encounter;"[7] and "while you are still on the way, fear not that you will die of thirst; for there are freshets of water prepared for children, the beginners on this path."[8]

Perhaps it would be better to speak of *paths* in the plural, if we are to remain true to the spirit of the Saint, who writes: "The Lord has different paths by which men may go to him, just as he also has many mansions."[9] Carmelite teaching allows us, then, to choose this or that preferred path for the divine encounter.

At the start we find a number of paths fairly well traced out; these correspond to what are called "methods of prayer" in other schools, though such terminology is not favored in Carmelite teaching. In the latter, "methods" are viewed as but different ways of loving, as crutches useful enough to a soul taking its first steps but destined to be cast aside as soon as the soul feels able to go on by itself. Or they may be treated like walking-sticks which some travelers like to

[7] *Way of Perfection*, chap XXI.
[8] *Ibid.* chap. XX.

93

keep with them, though they scarcely ever make use of them. Many Carmelite saints have begun their devotional journey in this way. St. Teresa, visiting her uncle at Hortigosa, received from him a book[10] of meditation at a time when she felt she "did not know how to pray properly" and, as she tells us, "I began . . . to start upon the way of prayer with this book for my guide."[11]

"Methods" then are not rejected by Carmelite teaching, at least so long as they arouse love in the soul and help the soul to encounter God, but all that savors of complication is. To be persuaded of this, we need only recall in how broad a sense both St. John of the Cross and St. Teresa conceived of meditation. According to them, it amounts to no more than a few simple questions with which the intellect occupies itself with regard to some imagined situation or concerning some mystery, the whole thing brought to a conclusion in loving quietude in God's presence.

According to the great Doctor of mystical the-

[10] *The Third Spiritual Alphabet* of Francisco de Osuna, of the Order of St. Francis.
[11] *Life*, chap. IV

ology, there are three parts to meditation. The first part pictures to the imagination, through some concrete image, the mystery of religion on which the mind is to linger. The second presents to the intellect the mystery thus represented in order that it may be plumbed. And the third part is a watchful and attentive waiting upon God: the soul gathers together the results of the two preceding steps and then "opens itself to the understanding of what God will make known to it." This is a truly simple path of prayer, but it conducts the soul in three simple stages from the representation, or image, to serious reality by means of the regulated use of the intellect. Such prayer is a kind of ladder which can lead the soul even to the threshold of the encounter with God, in which there occurs that revelation of divine light "which God will make known to it," as the text of St. John states.

It is interesting to note that this very simple method of prayer is in fundamental agreement with that which can be constructed from the remarks of St. Teresa on the same subject. She too suggests that we begin prayer by picturing to ourselves some mystery, most frequently an episode in the life of Jesus: for example, our Lord at the Pillar where he was scourged. We are to imagine this scene as taking place as close as possible to us, even within ourselves. Then, having fixed our imagination on the scene, we try to understand it by means of some simple thoughts about it: "It is well to reflect for a time and to think of the pains which He bore there, why He bore them, Who He is that bore them."[12] Finally, when the intellect has done its work, it is time for the use of the affective faculty: "We must not always tire ourselves by going in search of these ideas; we must remain by His side with our minds hushed in silence."[13] We thus come to that encounter spoken of by St. John of the Cross: *the door of the soul is open to what God will make known to it.*

Regrettably, these very direct styles of meditation were made slightly more complicated by later followers of St. Teresa and St. John of the Cross. These disciples suggest a division of the usual

[12] *Life*, chap. XIII; Peers I, 82.
[13] *Ibid.*

Carmelite prayer into six or even seven steps, according to the particular school of thought they follow. Yet even in these divisions, it is quite easy to discern the essential lines of the Teresian meditation. As the various parts are described in early Carmelite texts, they are:

Preparation: the sign of the Cross, the examination of conscience, and the Confiteor. This is the prelude to prayer as taught by St. Teresa herself.

Reading: This is the same step as that which John of the Cross and Teresa of Avila present to us as directed to the work of the imagination. For is not the end of reading to re-create before our eyes the mystery about which we are thinking, and to offer us a theme for our thoughts? From this, the mind raises itself up quite naturally to the more spiritual work of the meditation proper. This is the supreme moment when the understanding does its utmost to make its influence felt upon the will so that, as John of Jesus-Mary puts it, "the spark may ignite and burst into flame."

The soul then grows warm with love, and is prepared for the stage which the old authors describe as contemplation. Actually, this stage is identical with meditation or at least is never treated apart from it. Thus we find ourselves at the third stage of prayer, as it is explained by St. John of the Cross.

Other parts then follow—thanksgiving, offering, and petition. These are specific conclusions to the more general contemplation. But the distinction of all these is rather one of logic than of anything else; usually, they are not to be considered apart from contemplation proper. They represent motions of the soul; the words of *praise* issue from contemplation but are not of themselves sufficient, so acts are necessary as well. Hence the oblation or *offering* of self, which may be either total, or restricted to some particular point one may have promised to observe during the day: this latter is sometimes given the name of *resolution*. Finally, in the *petition*, one asks of God the special graces necessary to keep these promises as well as his help for other things.

John of Jesus-Mary—the father of this plan for meditation—realized it was not necessary for all these acts to be elicited in logical order. They may well be included in the course of the general prayer of contemplation, or even omitted should "the Spirit move us to more general motions of the soul." This admission has the basic effect of returning tacitly to the simple division of prayer into three parts as initially taught by St. John of the Cross and St. Teresa. And this, if there is any such thing, is the only "official" method of Carmel.

The majority of those who follow Carmelite teaching would be hard put to name any "official" method of prayer, no matter how broad its conceptions. There is just the compelling need to climb the mount of perfection, according to one's own manner of procedure—acting on one's own lights by oneself rather than following some beaten path. For this reason Carmelite authors frequently suggest other ways of prayer, all of them equally certain, by which souls can be united with God, ways leaving open to them the exercise of their personal initiative. We need not fear taking these paths, nor suffer any regret as though we were playing truant by thus wandering apart from the common course. Encouragement to do this very thing was in fact given by St. Teresa herself who was one of the first to feel this deep-seated need for freedom and to experiment with it. She often states that one ought to be somewhat original in prayer; the soul "should itself take note of what draws it most profitably, and thus learn to make use of varied paths."[14] She compares the soul to a spouse who, a while back, left her home: how complicated are the negotiations required before this situation can be remedied and she can be restored to her husband. To bring the soul to her own home again, we must use much adroitness and work gradually; otherwise, nothing will ever be accomplished. Similarly, thanks to "certain tendencies and certain endeavors, the soul is led little by little not to be afraid."[15]

Such liberty can also be justified in another way. The art of making use of every possible

[14] *Life*, chap. XIII; Peers I, 82.
[15] *Way of Perfection*, chap. XXVI; Peers II, 110.

means of being united with God, as it derives from this human flexibility, better prepares the soul to understand that other, supernatural flexibility which gives it over to the action of the Holy Spirit and his gifts. On this point St. Teresa insists that we leave the door open to the initiative of God in our prayers; and that, to do this, we should not shut ourselves up hermetically in ourselves, as if prayer were a one-sided business.

There are other ways as well by which we can be led to the longed-for encounter with God. One is simple reading, not undertaken as part of a method but done for its own sake. If we feel any false shame about making use of this means, then we need only recall that for many years it was Teresa's chief recourse when she "never dared begin to pray without a book;" for "when I had no book . . . my soul would at once become disturbed." Reading, she says, should be the recourse of the souls like hers to whom "God has not given . . . talents for reasoning with understanding or for making good use of the imagination."

Their way is a difficult one for, "if the master

who is directing them forbids them to read and thus find help for recollection, . . . prayer without this aid will be impossible for them to persist in for long." Moreover, the use of a book can be a wise thing, if it is done with freedom; but even so, it is only a means, "a companionship to me and a shield with which I could parry the blows of my many thoughts." It should then be treated as such, and not according to any fixed rule: "Sometimes I read a little, sometimes a great deal, according to the favor which the Lord showed me."[16] If we use this method, we should often lift our eyes from the book, using the words as a sort of springboard for faith to leap again into the quest for God. Once this encounter with him has been achieved, we close the book for it is no longer needed.

In addition to reading, devotional objects can likewise be of considerable help. Teresa did not hesitate to say: "You will find it very helpful if you can get an image or a picture of our Lord— one that you like."[17] Of course such an image

[16] *Life*, chap. IV; Peers I, 24-5.
[17] *Way of Perfection*, chap. XXVI; Peers II, 109.

ought to conform to good taste and to the right respect for the divine persons. If St. John of the Cross appears to have written a lot against images, this is because of the terrible abuses to which their use sometimes leads—when, for instance, they become nothing but "idols." But he writes in one place that "Images and portraits of the saints . . . are most important for divine worship and just as necessary to move the will to devotion." What he deprecates is the determined attachment to images as such—that spirit of ownership which is so often buried in their love, and which prevent the soul from taking "flight to God."[18]

This latter danger was foreseen by St. Teresa herself: "You have a representation of our Lord with you so that you may frequently converse with him, not just carry about with you, never looking at it."[19] When images or cards are made use of in this broad-minded way, they help some people to control their imaginations and thus indirectly aid them in recollection. No doubt St.

[18] *Ascent*, Bk. III, chap. XXXV, 4, 5, 6; Peers I, 292.
[19] *Way of Perfection*, chap. XXVI; Peers II, 109.

John of the Cross had this in mind when he sent his own drawing of Mount Carmel to some nuns.

After reading and devotional aids comes vocal prayer, which leads to an encounter with God just as efficaciously as any other means. "While you are saying the Lord's prayer or reciting some other words," says St. Teresa, it is quite possible for the Lord to grant you perfect contemplation."[20] Vocal prayer should not be rushed through, nor should it be mumbled but rather recited slowly and attentively. We should stop at any phrase or word which is to our special taste and then, if distractions arise, again take up the thread of the prayer. Of this Teresa did not hesitate to say that "if we pray in this manner, the prayer may be only vocal but the mind will be recollected much sooner.

St. John of the Cross was opposed to none of this, as one incident in his life clearly shows. There was a rather learned young man, a former student of law, who had entered the Carmelite Novitiate and who requested a certain book for use at meditation. John was the Rector of the place at this

[20] *Ibid.*, chap. XXVIII; Peers II, 115.

THE ENCOUNTER WITH GOD IN PRAYER

time, and replied to the request by sending a little
piece of paper. On this the novice was to write
the words of the Our Father, and meditate on
them for half an hour or so each day. Soon the
young man was seen praying with this piece of
paper in his hand, finding such joy in "decipher-
ing" the words that "tears flowed from his eyes
like little fountains." As John explained, what
we ask for in the Our Father sums up "all that is
necessary in order that the Eternal Father may
hear us."[21]

On her part, St. Thérèse of the Child Jesus seems
to say the same thing. "Sometimes, when I'm in
such a state of spiritual dryness that I can't find a
single thought in my mind which will bring me
close to God, I say an Our Father and a Hail
Mary very slowly indeed."[22]

Conversation with our Lord, unfettered by formalism of any kind and conducted in all simplicity,
seems to be the kind of prayer preferred by St.
Teresa, inasmuch as she considered prayer "nothing

[21] *Ascent*, Book III, XLIV, 4; Peers I, pp. 310-311.
[22] *Autobiography of St. Thérèse of Lisieux* (New York:
P. J. Kenedy and Sons, 1958) p. 290.

but friendly intercourse and frequent solitary converse with Him who we know loves us." Such conversation should be spontaneous: we should be ourselves, avoiding both the unnatural and the merely conventional. We must make our needs known to the Lord, showing ourselves to him as a familiar friend and not too much concerned about the form or the continuity of what we say: "Let them imagine themselves in the presence of Christ, and let them remain in converse with Him, without wearying their minds or fatiguing themselves by composing speeches to Him, but laying their needs before Him."[23] This kind of conversation knows many loving looks in which we dwell upon the thought of Christ, and long spaces of silence as well. We ought, moreover, not to speak to Him only of what affects ourselves directly; we should above all speak of whatever concerns Him, and let Him look after our affairs. How often St. Teresa seems ready to stop in the middle of her prayer in order to express such thoughts as these: "I am ashamed, Lord,

[23] *Life*, chap. XIII; Peers I, 7-8. See also St. Augustine's Confessions, X, 22-30.

when I see thee in such a plight. . . . Let us both go together on this single path, Lord, for whither thou goest, I must go."[24] Again, we ought sometimes to be still, enjoying the happiness of being in his Company: "We must sometimes remain by his side with our minds hushed in silence. If we can, we should occupy ourselves in looking upon Him who is looking at us; keep Him Company."[25]

There are even shorter paths than these conversations and glances: they can be called attitudes of the soul. Because they require so little human effort, beginners don't think they are forms of prayer at all; but they can, nevertheless, be put to great use by those who find them suitable, even for the whole period they remain. If we distinguish between them, following the text of this or that Carmelite saint, it is only for the sake of explaining them clearly; actually, they more or less overlap.

On some days we should prepare for prayer with the chief thought of being on the alert *to hear God or our Lord*, without saying anything

[24] *Way of Perfection*, chap. XXVI; Peers II, 108
[25] *Life*, chap. XIII; Peers I, 83.

ourselves. We shouldn't weary or trouble ourselves trying to arouse too much feeling or enthusiasm, for this is to be wanting in simplicity.
Rather we should place ourselves silently in God's
presence and, as St. John of the Cross says: "Memory should be still and dumb, and the ear of the
spirit . . . attentive in silence to God alone, saying
with the Prophet, 'Speak, Lord, for thy servant
heareth.' "

If listening to God be a good method, it is also
well to devote at least some of our time to *looking*
at him. St. Teresa has suggested our use of this
method: "Your spouse never takes his eyes off
you, daughters. . . . Right now, He is only waiting
for us to look at Him." Christ submits Himself,
so to speak, to the motions and desires of our souls.
"He becomes subject to us and is pleased to let you
be the mistress and to conform to your will. If
you are happy, look upon your risen Lord. . . .
How bright and beautiful He was then, how ma-
jestic! . . . If you are suffering trials or are sad,
look upon Him on his way to the Garden. . . . He
will look upon you with His lovely and compas-

sionate eyes, and in comforting your grief will forget His own."[26]

Almost identical advice is given by St. John of the Cross: "Have a loving attentiveness to God, with no desire to feel or understand anything in particular concerning Him."[27] In this connection, it is interesting to note that Paul Claudel spontaneously reverted to this manner of praying:

"I am come, O my Mother, just to look at you;
  Just to look, and to weep in joy, for that I know
  Myself to be your son, and you to be where you
    are. . . .
  Happy am I, O Mary, to be with you in your own
    house,
  Needing no words, but seeing your face,
  The while my heart metely hymns your praise."[28]

There is also another method of prayer suggested by John of Saint-Sampson, and of which he speaks in treating of the presence of God. According to him, it is the aspiration to God which constitutes the essential element in prayer and he distinguishes these degrees: "to offer oneself and

[26] *Way of Perfection*, chap. XXVI; Peers II, 107-8.
[27] *Points of Love*, n. 9; Peers III, 227.
[28] Paul Claudel, *Ecoute ma fille*: La Vierge à Midi, p. 34.

all created things to God . . . to ask His gifts in Him and for His own sake, to conform onself to His will in complete and whole-hearted sincerity; and finally, to unite oneself to Him, thus by transcendence embodying all that has gone before, and in the highest degree."[29] It is not necessary to insist on this manner of prayer; but there are certain days and times when it is advisable to place oneself before God, wholly intent on "flowing back" to him, wholly determined in our desires to turn back to our eternal source of life and being, resolved to offer ourselves entirely to Him just like a drop of dew offers itself to the morning sun which causes it to evaporate and return to the aery spaces from which it had fallen.

To sum up: we ought to foster in our hearts a universal sense of God's presence. During the whole of his life, Lawrence of the Resurrection practiced this kind of prayer and it led him to a pinnacle: "My usual practice is to remain in the presence of God with all the humility of a useless but faithful servant. . . . From the beginning of

[29] *La Doctrine* . . . , p. 137.

my novitiate ... I have studied to convince myself of the truth of this Divine Being rather by
the light of faith than by the labor of meditation
and reading."[30] He nevertheless knew every one
of the difficulties that we all encounter, for as He
himself told us: "often in the beginning, I passed
the whole time of prayer just rejecting distractions
and falling into them again."[31] But later he discovered his own personal way of going to God
and gently maintained his course on it to the very
end: the encounter with his God.

This encounter is the culmination, the fulfillment of any one of those paths along which prayer
can lead us. Different as they may appear, they all
lead to this summit through whatever means and
inspirations are available, through whatever prep-
arations precede. There, for the period of prayer,
the soul is set in God's presence where great
quietude and interior peace prevail, where the soul
is illumined by searching rays of divine light and
inspiration. It is to these heights that the saints of
Carmel all try to lead us, wisely telling us that

[30] *Practice of the Presence* of God, pp. 20-1.
[31] *Ibid.* p. 71.

when we have come to this state of prayer, we have already completed our journey, we are already face to face with God. In the eyes of Thérèse of Lisieux, prayer was no more than "a launching out of the heart, a lifting up of one's eyes, a cry." [32] What could be more simple, more spontaneous—and yet what defies analysis more than these? Here, in this apex of man's effort to pray, the encounter with God is achieved: now it is God alone who can fulfill this work in the soul which has become passive under His hand.

It is of course essential to note, for a precise understanding of the matters we are dealing with here, one point: while the diverse paths of prayer all terminate in the same encounter with God, they do so only because they are all parts of another, a larger and more important Way: Christ. "Progress comes not except through the imitation of Christ . . . and no man comes to the Father but by Him. . . . For as he says: 'I am the door; by me if any man enter in he shall be saved.' " [33] It is hardly necessary to insist that it is Christ himself

[32] *Autobiography*, chap. XXXVII; Knox, p. 289.
[33] *Ascent*, Bk. II, chap. VII, 8; Peers, I, 86.

who is the path to God, the open door to him, the "Way."

And St. Mary Magdelene de' Pazzi says: "At the same time that Christ is our path, he is also the guide who leads the traveler on it. . . . For my Word is not satisfied to make of himself your way, in order that He may lead you to me. He wishes as well to be your guide, so that in fixing your eyes on Him to follow Him, you may one day come to rest in the Father, the Son, and the Holy Spirit. But take note that the guide who has gone before you in power is taking giant steps: *exultavit ut gigas ad currendam viam.* If, then, you do not wish to lose sight of him quickly, you must make haste." [34]

These important words imply serious consequences. They tell us that all prayer of whatever sort is worthless, unless it is founded "on the living rock which is Christ." We should therefore never be presumptuous enough to think that we might abandon our Lord's companionship. This is the universal teaching of the Saints; and they frequently tell us, St. Teresa among them, that the

[34] Sainte Marie-Madeleine de' Pazzi, *Oeuvres*, t. II, p. 253.

subtle temptation to strive for perfection apart from Christ has caused much harm. Christ alone can give meaning and purpose to the different paths of prayer: these latter are in fact nothing but ramifications of the one great "Way."

Our meditations then should be founded on the mysteries of either our Lord's life or that of his mother. We need but the merest touch of earthly background, mainly from the gospel; and the play of the imagination should be more and more narrowed so that we may lovingly savor the core of the mystery, thus entering more quickly into this "cavern of rock." [35] Through Christ we will thus enter the mysterious life of God, into knowledge of the Trinity; it is by Him, in Him, and with Him that we shall do so; for to Him alone has been given authority to guide us, in the deepest sense of the word, to God. Were we to trust to our own efforts and to reject his aid or ignore it, we would certainly be courting disaster.

If we should need books for our meditations, the work should by preference be one that will

[35] *Spiritual Canticle*, (A), Stanza XXXVII.

put us in immediate touch with our Lord. The *Imitation* of course is an excellent one; but the Gospels are unparalleled, and to read the Gospel is to penetrate into knowledge of Christ most directly. Contemplatives feel they are "drinking fulsome draughts of their well-beloved" [36] whenever they refresh themselves at this spring, which in fact becomes their very life and soul, and they end by finding little use for any other book in comparison to this one which contains all. As St. Teresa said: "I have always been more fond of the words of the gospel and have found more recollection in them than in the most carefully planned books." [37] Thérèse of Lisieux tells us the same and at the close of her life she wrote: "I have found less than nothing in books; for me the Gospel is all that I need.[38]

If it is vocal prayer on which we mainly rely, there too Christ has shown us the way. Certainly the more simple and meaningful prayers are the Our Father, which our Lord Himself has taught

[36] *Spiritual Canticle* (A), Stanza XVII, 4-8.
[37] *Way of Perfection*, chap. XXI; Peers II, 90.
[38] *L'Esprit de Ste. Therese de Lisieux*, p. 185.

us, and the Hail Mary whose first part comes from the Gospel. In these, and in all forms of prayer, let Christ be at their center; let us never turn aside from him, either when we speak or when we listen, waiting with patience for his words to our soul. As Thérèse of Lisieux says: "Jesus doesn't need to make use of books or teachers in the instruction of souls; isn't He the teacher of all teachers, conveying knowledge with never a word spoken?" [39]

We will learn from him and find quiet peace and love before the tabernacle where he is present; or, if we are occupied in his work, by total abandonment to His redeeming love.

The Encounter With God

John of Saint-Sampson tells us that "the path and indeed the whole study of those who ardently and lovingly wish to attain to an encounter with God is in prayer. By it, "he writes," they readily mount to their meeting with Him." [40]

[39] *Autobiography*, Knox. trans., p. 218-19.
[40] *La Doctrine* . . . , p. 175.

As we have seen, this meeting with God is an accomplished fact in the lives of those who pray well. We have been observing different descriptions of prayer, seeing our various ways of praying and examining paths rather than the goals to which they lead. In actual fact, however, we already find God, we already meet Him, as soon as we begin to seek; or as Pascal wisely discerned, we do not even begin to seek him unless He is already found. Of course this is done in a halting, incomplete way and according to our faltering dispositions at the start; but as St. Teresa noted, even before reaching the fountain of contemplation where they may slake their thirst completely, contemplatives are partially satisfied by "freshets of water" they are given on the way. Thus, even at the beginning, we can savor God, we can experience Him in some way—a fact that, in Carmelite teaching, is attributed much significance, for we believe that even the search itself for God is a special grace infused by Him.

Still, we know that of ourselves we could never attain to union with God: we lack both the skill and even the knowledge of the means to attain contemplation in Him. In this regard, St. Teresa has made some very accurate observations on certain contemplatives who even, apparently, arrested their processes of breathing in order to prolong of to facilitate contemplative prayer: "Persons in this state prefer the body to remain motionless, for otherwise their peace would be destroyed; for this reason they do not stir. Speaking is a distress to them. . . . They are tempted to believe they can prolong (their delight) and some of them even try not to breathe. This is ridiculous. . . . The most we can do to prolong this favor of God is to realize that we can neither diminish nor add to it." [41]

A Carmelite nun, Sister Marie of Saint Joseph, wrote a humorous dialogue in which she slyly mocks one such well-meaning, but ill-advised, "contemplative." The name of the latter is Justa and she speaks thus in Sister Marie's report: "Once the meditation has been finished, I try to pass on to contemplation. Here indeed I encounter some difficulties! I close my eyes; I strain all efforts to put every faculty to rest; and sometimes it seems to

[41] *Way of Perfection*, chap. XXXI; Peers II, 128-9.

me that even my breathing interferes with the rest I seek, which I consider to be actual contemplation; so then I hold my breath." It is laughable to think people should have aspired to true contemplation in this way; God would doubtless refuse himself to anyone who undertook to follow such a misguided method.

Yet those who follow Carmelite spirituality, without straining after such eccentricities as these, certainly have the right to hope for a satisfying, even delectable, encounter with God. And St. John of the Cross, in commenting on our Lord's words "Knock and it shall be opened to you," promises it: "Seek in reading and thou shalt find in meditation; knock in prayer and it shall be opened to you in contemplation." [42]

The Saint also tells us that it is God who takes the first step: "Thou showest thyself first of all and goest out to meet them that desire thee." [43] He goes forward in search of the soul; He knows how to handle each of its strivings in a wonderful way. And He leads the soul by a marvellous

[42] *Points of Love*, n. 64; Peers III, 233.
[43] *Spiritual Sentences and Maxims*, n. 2; Peers III, 219.

uplifting process from earlier feeling of sensible delight to the more substantial and secret relations it will enjoy in His own high friendship.

He shows himself at first with all the love of a mother, in order to encourage the soul to push onward. Were the soul not thus enticed by perceptive consolations, it might become afraid and stop short. God thus deals very gently with it, caressing it "as is the tender child by its loving mother who . . . murtures it with sweet milk and soft and pleasant food, and carries it and caresses it in her arms." [44] This indescribable tenderness is very helpful to the beginner who feels buoyed up, comforted, and begins to savor the path of prayer it has chosen or may even try them all with varying feelings of pleasure. In the very midst of these delights, the soul is given "little morsels of contemplation," as St. John of the Cross calls them.

But if the soul travels willingly to meet the Lord, it is not satisfied with the "freshets of water" it meets on the way; it ardently desires to come to that great fountain—the great and noble encounter of true contemplation. This time, God

[44] *Dark Night*, I, II, 2; Peers I, 330.

draws the soul to himself rather than stoops down
to its level: "it is no longer the soul that receives
aught, but rather it is itself received into the
spirit." [45]

If the soul is to attain this encounter, it must
undergo some deprivation: "As the child grows
bigger, the mother gradually ceases caressing it
and, hiding her tender love, puts bitter aloes under
her sweet breast, sets down the child from her
arms and makes it walk upon its feet, so that it
may lose the habits of a child and betake itself
to more important and substantial occupations." [46]
The Lord hides Himself and allows the soul to
walk by itself along a path which speedily becomes steeper. Alone, the soul bitterly misses the
friend who had so lightened the steps of the journey and who, without almost any effort on its
own part, had opened to it the scriptures, expos-
ing one after another of its treasures.

The soul thus looks about anxiously for a being
constantly slipping away from it—or at least
slipping away as the loving mother but gradually

[45] *Ibid.*, I, IV, 2; Peers I, 339
[46] *Ibid.* I, I, 2; Peers I, 330.

making itself felt under this or that guise until they too slip away, and the soul goes on in its quest for God in a purer form. Now is the time for it to select a more direct path: a path in which prayer is simpler, barer—like the slow readings that have already been described, the mere looking at God with great love, the patient attentiveness to hear what God himself may wish to say.

This is a wearisome and uneventful part of the journey. The soul moves in an arid desert. It is desolate, fearing that the meeting with God may never come about. But even in such fear the soul is already experiencing God.

For the assurance of those who fear that they may be wasting their time at prayer, it should be recalled that the greatest contemplatives are often those who journey along in dryness, whom God sometimes allows to think that they do not even know how to pray. St. Teresa, for example, thought of herself as inferior to other souls because she was unable to meditate: "God had not given me talents for reasoning with the understanding or for making good use of the imagination: my imagination is so poor that even when

I thought about the Lord's humanity, or tried to imagine it to myself, as I was in the habit of doing, I never succeeded. And although, if they persevere, people may attain more quickly to contemplation by following this method of not laboring with the understanding, it is a very troublesome and painful process." [47] Lawrence of the Resurrection has told us that he never knew how to pray, at least according to the stricter rules and that he was never so dry as during the times of retreat. And here is something even more consoling: Thérèse of Lisieux never felt much attraction for "involved prayers," and many times wrote of her aridity as the "daily bread of bitter dryness." [48] But who can doubt that souls like hers, even when they feel themselves to be the driest, are already close to God?

We cling to God in greater purity of faith when we are not sensible of His presence, for then we have gone beyond the "ignoble way" of loving him. The encounter with him takes place, so to speak, in a haze; without having drawn attention

[47] *Life*, chap. IV; Peers I, 24.
[48] *Autobiography* 185, 198-9, 228, 254-7, 289-90.

to himself, Christ has "passed in haste" beside the soul, "scattering a thousand graces" upon it. This inception of contemplative activity is so delicate a thing that it defies our notice: the clear rays of divine light are unseen. It is like "a delicate, aery vapor which ascends from the warm fire of meditation."

In this state, the soul neither sees nor feels anything different, but it should judge its prayer with good sense, according to the fruit it produces. Does the soul find itself preoccupied, even slightly, during the time of prayer? Does it find itself, the prayer accomplished, nourished and willing to do good? If so, then there has been an encounter with God. If not, then let the soul examine itself with as much accuracy as possible regarding its conduct during the day.

There are certain signs listed by John of the Cross and others as decisively marking the steps between meditation and contemplation, and no doubt the most important of them are the intensified desire to do God's work, an increased mistrust of worldly ways that are not in accord with Christian life and a greater desire for recollection.

Such signs justify the soul in concluding that God has been found.

Finally, the day comes when this encounter with God is actually felt by the soul. The soul has grown accustomed to its new way of loving God and of cleaving to Him, of hearing His voice within itself. For God speaks to those he loves "like a good Shepherd; with a call so gentle that even they can hardly recognize it, He teaches them to know His voice." [49] This marks the conscious beginning of the contemplative life: "a door is opened in heaven" (Apoc. 4:1), and the soul is bidden to cross its threshold and to find Him whom it thought lost on the way.

Christ can no longer hide himself: it grieves him too much to behold the anxious searching of the soul that He loves. He thus allows it to taste the sweet satisfaction of a new encounter by establishing it, a little at a time, in a state of prayer which St. Teresa describes as the prayer of quietude: "This state is a recollecting of the faculties within the soul, so that its fruition of that content-

[49] St. Teresa, *Interior Castle*, Fourth Mansions, chap. III; Peers II, 240.

ment may be of greater delight. But the faculties are not lost nor do they sleep. The will alone is occupied, and in such a way that, without knowing it, it becomes captive. It allows itself to be imprisoned by God, as one who well knows itself to be the captive of Him who loves it." [50]

But the divine grasp it still a relaxed one; the soul can still withdraw into itself and there is no doubt that it should sometimes do so to struggle with its own imagination or reason, which are much less subdued than the will. The soul knows nevertheless that it is through this supernatural repose that it encounters God. The soul has found him and this time it is aware of the fact and will cling to him. "God, of his greatness, desires the soul to realize that his majesty is so near it that it need not send him messengers. . . . It could not possibly decide that God is not with it." [51]

There are thus two characteristics in this kind of prayer—ones which, in higher forms of prayer, attain richer development still. These are a certain

[50] *Life, chap. XIV*; Peers I, 83.
[51] St. Teresa, *Life*, chaps. XIV, XV; Peers I, 85-95.

suspension of feeling, and an actual experience of God's presence.

God will give himself to the soul even more fully than hitherto as a consequence of these new alternations of encounter and watchful questing. He will not be satisfied just to approach the soul in a hidden manner, as during the period of dryness; He will not be satisfied merely to spend a while, of whatever length, beside the soul; He wishes to be closely united with the soul. And one might say that he no longer witholds anything.

This is that "union" which St. Teresa permits us to long for because its effects are so helpful to us. "What a great reward this is," she exclaims, "for even a moment of it suffices to recompense the soul for all the trials it can possibly have endured. While seeking God in this way, the soul becomes conscious that it is fainting almost completely away, in a kind of swoon, with an exceeding great and sweet delight. It gradually ceases to breathe and . . . all outward strength vanishes, while the strength of the soul increases." [52] Now is the encounter with God clearly realized: all

[52] *Life*, chap. XVIII; Peers I, 108-109.

the forces of the soul's being are fused in Christ who, speaking to St. Teresa of this state, says: "It is no longer itself that lives; but I." [53]

Such is the bipolarity of the prayer of union: a suspension of all human activity, and a living certitude of God's presence within the soul. Even should the soul be called to a mystic vocation marked by raptures and ecstasies, there would only be a slight difference of degree between this grand encounter with God and the immediate contacts of the other. But these latter are special graces about which we should feel more wonder than desire, for in their regard no wish of ours will ever hasten God's hand. They are a matter of God's own choosing.

Finally, almost inaccessibly above us, there is that lasting union with God which St. Teresa described as a "marriage"—a union entirely of the spirit because it makes of the soul an entity entirely one with God in spirit. At such a height, the spouse of God again experiences divine gifts which raise it above the mortal state, at least for a time. John of the Cross has given us descriptions

[53] *Ibid.*; Peers I, 110.

of these interior visitations of the soul by the Holy Ghost, and he calls them *encounters*. "To the end that it may be more completely perfected and raised up above the flesh, God makes upon the soul assaults that are glorious and Divine and that take place after the manner of encounters, . . . wherewith he penetrates the soul continually, deifying its substance. . . . The reason for this is that God has encountered the soul and pierced it to the quick in the Holy Spirit." [54]

But even with these graces the soul is not satisfied! How wide are the horizons which this declaration opens before us. Raised to a state of deification such as St. John describes in his *Spiritual Canticle*, the soul still sighs after God and beseeches Him "to break the web of this sweet encounter." [55] It longs, in short, to die. Only this can break the tenuous links which bind flesh and spirit. And when that filmy veil, through which there has already streamed the first rays of glory, shall be rent, then there will follow that final and

[54] *Living Flame*, stanza I, 35.
[55] Ibid., stanza I, 29-36.

lasting encounter between God and the soul—one which has been sought unremittingly in silent hours of earthly prayer and which will endure forever.

5

Fidelity in Little Things

W E WILL make more rapid progress in the life of prayer if we learn to make the most prudent use of the so-called little things in our lives. Be they small or great, no details of daily life should be allowed to challenge the universal sway of love which, for all its concern with broad principles and systematization, is rooted in our everyday activities, incarnated in them. St. Teresa categorically affirms this in enumerating the excuses made by certain nuns about matters concerned with priority and precedence: "You will say that these are little things which have to do with human nature and are not worth troubling about; do not trifle with them, for . . . they spread like foam on water, and there is no small matter so extremely dangerous."[1]

Nothing is a trifle, or could be so, when great matters are at stake: this is the principle that should guide us in connection with matters involving the so-called little things—insignificant duties, slight acts of renunciation, the little sufferings and joys which fill each of our days and which to the bystander might seem unimportant. They are far from being so, however, especially when they are viewed in the light of our spiritual progress. In that regard they can be obstacles to the love of God or sources of deception in the expression of that love; or, on the contrary, instruments in helping us love God more and even reflections, in a way, of that great love in which God holds the entire world.

Little Things as Obstacles to the Love of God

Carmelite spirituality has some very fundamental things to say about the importance of even the small details of our daily life; and it does not shrink

[1] *Way of Perfection*, chap. XII; Peers II, 52.

from telling us how serious damage can come to our devotional life if these things are not seen in their proper light.

"Nothing is a little thing when the danger is so great." This dictum of St. Teresa is a sort of resume of all the prudent observations which the Carmelite mystics have given us regarding the regulation of our dealings with created things. "Where thy treasure is, there is thy heart also," as our Lord pointed out; and if this statement is valid with regard to the treasures which we store up in heaven through the merits of our accumulated good works, it likewise has a great deal of bearing on our tendencies to become inordinately attached to possessions. How easy it is for "men's hearts to fall from their high estate and to become debased if they lower themselves to put their trust in the children of men!" This ancient declaration from *The Institution of the First Monks* tells us of the antiquity of the problem we are discussing and long antedates anything John of the Cross wrote on the subject.

Yet to John of the Cross belongs the merit of having thrown precise and definitive light upon this question. His conception of the matter is quite exact: *No one will normally attain to contemplation and to real union with God who knowingly and deliberately cherishes an attachment to any creature whatsoever.* However slight such an attachment might be, it will still be enough to impede the flight of the soul. It will, so to speak, defile the soul with respect to God to whom the soul wishes to be united.

In his *Ascent of Mount Carmel,* the Saint asks: *whether it be necessary for the soul to mortify its desires, howsoever trifling they may appear to be?* He does this in order to refute the objection of those who say that attention to the mere details of daily living has little to do with our progress in the spiritual life. Here is his categorical response to the question: "All the . . . voluntary desires, whether they be of mortal sin, which are the gravest, or of venial sin, which are less grave, or whether they be only of imperfections, which are the least grave of all, must be driven away every one, and the soul must be free of them all, howsoever slight they may be, if it is to come to this complete union; and the reason is . . . if this soul wills any imperfection which God wills not, there would not be made one will of God, since the soul would have a will for that which God has not." [2]

The Holy Doctor does not hesitate to give precise details about apparent trifles which can become obstacles in the path of love unless we have the strength to break with them: "Of the voluntary desires which, though they be for very small things, are . . . intentional venial sin, any one which is not conquered suffices to impede union. . . . These habitual imperfections are, for example, a common custom of much speaking, or some slight attachment which we never quite wish to conquer—such as that to a person, a garment, a book, a cell, a particular kind of food, tittle-tattle, fancies for tasting, knowing or hearing certain things and suchlike." [3]

It thus happens that even a very small thing is enough to fetter the soul, to make it like "the fly that clings to honey" or "the bird held by a slender cord" which imprisons it so that it cannot

[2] I, XI, 2, 3; Peers I, 49.
[3] *Ascent* I, XI, 3, 4.

135

fly. In this way our enthusiasm is shackled; bars are set before the entrance to the sweet and welcoming house of contemplation. Very often this is the basic cause of our aridity and of our lack of fervor for the things that are God's. We know very well how he requires us to make a sacrifice of all these things . . . but we try to pretend that we do not realize this. We even go further. We drag ourselves along half-heartedly because we did not have the courage to cut to the quick right away; but then, after having tried countless other ways of escaping our responsibility, we find that one day we must do away with the obstacle, break the thread, if we are to go forward.

Perhaps we murmur over this, like certain of Christ's disciples: "This saying is hard, and who can hear it?" It is nevertheless a fact and one which Carmelite mystics propose for our consideration only after they had the courage to practice it in their own lives.

On this matter, St. Teresa is in agreement with St. John of the Cross. She writes: "Unless we take great care and each of us looks well to it that she renounce her self will, which is the most important business of all, there will be many things to deprive us of the holy freedom of spirit which our souls seek in order to soar to their maker.[4] This is very close to the figure which St. John of the Cross used when he spoke of the bird which must fly quickly to God.

Another sentence tells us more of this: "With regard to small things we must be very careful, as soon as we begin to grow fond of them, to withdraw our thoughts from them and turn them to God." [5] St. Teresa speaks in her most characteristic vein, however, when she uses her own favorite images: "If we fill the palace of the soul with vulgar people and all kinds of junk, how can the Lord and his court occupy it?" [6]

In support of this doctrine, we may also cite St. Thérèse of the Child Jesus as she laments the souls of religious and lay people alike who waste their time and energies over trifles. "Oh! that there were not so many religious who do almost nothing and say: 'I am not obliged to do this or that . . . After

---

[4] *Way of Perfection*, c. X; Peers II, 42.
[5] *Ibid.*, Peers II, 43.
[6] *Ibid.*, c. XXVIII; Peers II, 118.

all, there is no great harm done if I chat here for a while or if I rest and so on and on.' How few are the souls who really perform every good action that is possible to them." [7] As she saw things, we must be constantly on guard if our hearts are to be free. Such was the fruit of her experience. "In this, as in all else, I must practice sacrifice and self-denial. When I write a letter I feel it will produce no fruit unless it cost an effort and the effort be made out of obedience. So, too, when I am talking with a novice, I am ever on the watch to mortify myself, avoiding all questions which would tend to gratify my curiosity." [8]

These passages underline the perils to which we are exposed in our dealings over little things. They also remind us that we ought to direct ourselves according to large-minded views and with great flexibility, to avoid any exaggerated emphasis on minutiae. The Carmelite saints who are so careful about details are not trying to create a counting-house atmosphere in our thinking about heavenly things, or to turn our spiritual lives into a balance

[7] Cited by Père Petitot, O. P., *Sainte Thérèse de Lisieux* (Paris: Desclee), p. 41.
[8] *Autobiography*, cii, p. 177.

sheet with credits on one side, debits on the other. They are concerned with trifles only insofar as these latter get in the way of our loving God, and with the spirit of mortification only as an instrument of greater divine love.

Little Things as Deceptions in our Love of God

When we have overcome the first danger to our growth in divine love, a second peril confronts us. This one emerges with the keen sense of disappointment we feel regarding the trifles that seem to make up our lives; we sometimes feel that these little things can't really serve as a means by which we can show our love of God. Don't we sometimes deceive ourselves by believing that divine love must be shown in remarkable occurrences rather than in the small details of daily life?

Even in the affairs of the mystical life, there is a difference between actual reality and our dream of it. How often we deceive ourselves with adolescent dreams bursting with enthusiasm, and how often the bubble breaks under the recurring, unavoidable attacks of a harsh reality! How often can we say of our lives what Eve said of the serpent: "he deceived me! ?"

There is a parable in the gospel which doubtless captures this disappointment better than any other text: "Men . . . are like to children sitting in the marketplace and speaking one to another, and saying: we have piped to you and you have not danced, we have mourned and you have not wept" (Luke 7:32). The reality and the dream do not jibe; the soul thirsts to do great things, and life offers it nothing more than a round of colorless, monotonous trifles. And the soul, failing to discern the greatness which can be had in the faithful accomplishment of little things, draws poison from its dream by taking refuge in a denial of what is real.

This is too often the case in the spiritual life: noble aspirations to perfection become frustrated in the details of everyday activity, and souls otherwise possessed by good will take refuge in an ivory tower. And even if these details of daily life do not actually become obstacles to loving God, they sometimes turn out to be constant sources of disillusionment.

To dispel the misunderstandings here, we should consider the examples given us by the saints. Their voluntary self-effacement shows us how we should not allow ourselves to be worn out by commonplace things. In spite of all the trivial details they had to encounter and overcome, their hearts remained great. Teresa of Avila dreamed of being a martyr when she was a child and set out to fulfill her divine dream in life. "All that the soul can do for God seems to it slight by comparison with its desires," she wrote.[9]

Similar aspirations preoccupied St. Therese of the Child Jesus. "I feel as if I were called to be a fighter, a priest, an apostle, a doctor, a martyr; as if I could never satisfy the needs of my nature without performing . . . every kind of heroic action at once. I feel as if I'd got the courage to be a crusader . . . dying on the field of battle for the defense of the Church." [10] This is true enthusiasm, for it does not yield in the face of a monotonous and colorless reality.

Such mystics as Saint Thérèse never allow

[9] *Interior Castle*, Fifth Mansions, c. II; Peers II, 255.
[10] *Autobiography*, c. 30 p. 233.

themselves to be deceived by trifles. They know how to set those trifles in the framework of a larger reality, thus transforming them into occasions for showing their love of God. Thus they joyfully spent their lives in work which of itself was often wearisome and went unnoticed. Sometimes it is good to think of what actually occupied the saints when they were at their daily tasks rather than as they are hieratically posed on the altars or in niches about the church.

As a foundress, St. Teresa probably touched the heights of human greatness. Yet she generously performed the lowliest of tasks. "At St. Joseph's Convent in Avila," we are told by one of the nuns who lived with her, "there were at first no lay sisters, and each of the choir nuns took her weekly tour of duty in the kitchen. In spite of her many duties, our holy mother fulfilled this task like the rest of us. How great was our joy to see her in the kitchen! There she performed her work with much cheerfulness and the fullest desire to do well by all of us." [11] At Malagon, "the holy mother could be found from daybreak until late

[11] *Foundations*, t. III, p. 505.

at night among the workmen all during the time the monastery was being built. She was the first one to snatch up the broom and the dust-pan."

St. John of the Cross, when the Convent at Granada was being founded, worked bareheaded under the sun, carrying stones to help the masons.

St. Mary Magdalene de' Pazzi assumed the most difficult tasks in the convent. One day, while she was washing clothes, she fell into ecstasy and later had to break the water which had frozen around her hands.

Lawrence of the Resurrectoin worked in the kitchen of his monastery, or even went painfully to Burgundy to purchase supplies of wine for the community; and "this was very trying to him because he was lame in one leg." Finally, he was assigned "to the shoe-repair shop where he liked it very much." [12]

And what were the tasks which awaited St. Thérèse of the Child Jesus in the Carmel of her dreams which she entered as a teenage girl. She swept the cloister, she did the washing, and she helped an infirm old nun hobble into the refec-

[12] *Practice of the Presence of God*, p. 69.

tory.[13] No doubt these are minor details, but they are also richly suggestive, telling us how generous souls possessed of the highest aspirations were able to spend their lives in wearisome and routine tasks. And they did this without feeling in the least disgruntled; for they knew how to make the most of the slightest trifles, being convinced that true love will not allow itself to be hindered by any obstacle whatever.

In considering these things, dare we complain? May we allow our noblest desires to shrivel up because there are petty details and little insignificant happenings in our lives? Should we not, on the contrary, strive to gain possession of those secret means which will prevent us from being deceived by the seeming pettinesses of life and thereby allow us to build up our great reward in heaven?

Little Things As Occasions for Great Love

Little things can serve as much as big ones to provide love with occasions, almost infinite in their scope, for love to express itself and to prove itself. It is true that there is no greater love than that which lays down its life for a friend (John 15:13), but which manifestation of such love is greater: the one that immolates itself all at once on the field of battle, or one that sacrifices itself a little at a time, drop by drop so to speak, in the abnegations of daily life. This latter method is a real holocaust of the self: "The life of one who wishes to be among the closest friends of God is one long martyrdom," [13] says St. Teresa. This is also the most frequent kind of martyrdom, and one which the great saints understood better than any other. As St. Thérèse of Lisieux said: "Sensational acts of piety are not for me. . . . Well, even a little child can scatter flowers. . . . That shall be my life . . . to miss no single opportunity of making some small sacrifice. . . . always doing the tiniest thing right, and doing it for love." [14]

In this way the soul, without relinquishing its limitless desires, learns to find God in little things in place of big ones. And is not God truly there?

[13] *Way of Perfection*, c. XII; Peers II, 50.
[14] *Autobiography*, Knox p. 237.

According to Pascal, there are two infinities: "one is that of greatness, the other of littleness. Inasmuch as we ourselves transcend little things, we fancy ourselves capable of encompassing them; yet as much power is necessary to become nothing as to become everything. One depends upon the other and one leads to the other." It takes almost greater genius in fact to discern the infinitude of littleness, inasmuch as it is less evident to our senses, it breaks with lesser eclat over us. In this sense Thérèse of Lisieux was a genius, and they said of her in the *Procedure of Canonization*: "it seems that she has concealed her strength in a multitude of tiny, even microscopic acts." She utilized the infinitude of daily life which we fail to evaluate correctly—the realm of little, trifling, tiny things where she was queen: "a very insignificant person who can't offer to God anything but very insignificant sacrifices," [15] as she described herself in writing of some of her mortifications, such as putting up with an old nun who continually rattled her rosary, or allowing herself to be

[15] *Autobiography*, c. 38, p. 299.

splashed with water while the wash was being done.

"I tried my best to do good on a small scale. . . . I would fold up the mantles which the sisters had left lying about, and make myself useful in ways of that sort."[16] It is very touching to see Thérèse of Lisieux repeating the acts of love of St. Teresa of Avila several centuries before: "When evening had come, as the holy mother told us, and she had completed her examination of conscience, she realized that she had not performed any work of charity on that day. She went therefore to the choir to mend the cloaks she found in the closet. . . . At other times she would take a little lamp and station herself on the stairs to light the way down the steps for the sisters and for all who needed it."[17]

It is of such trifles that life is made. What opportunities they offer us to show love of God—a love that shall be various and sensitively proportioned to each occasion. How great the number of little acts, of little sorrows occurring within a

[16] *Ibid.* p. 196.
[17] *Foundations*, p. 575.

single day that afford us the chance to express greater love through them to God, or at least to bear them more willingly. In these matters we have an opportunity to love infinitely—and one which is just as great as if we were occupied in great affairs of state or other matters of importance.

Consider once more the Gospel. Our Lord condemned the sterile formalism of the Pharisees who, because they were enamoured of small observances done for their own sake, lost the sense of their meaning and purpose and let them become obstacles to religious life. He told us the story of the prodigal son who, in the weariness and apparent monotony of his life, aspired to adventure but encountered nothing more than disappointment and rebuffs. But he also spoke of the greatness of humble things, the smallest matters, the jot and tittle of the law (Matt. 5:18). "Woe to him that shall break one of these least commandments. . . (he) shall be called the least in the kingdom of heaven (Matt. 5:19). The faithful servant, on the contrary, will be rewarded: "Because thou hast been faithful over a few things,

I will place thee over many things" (Matt. 25:
21, 23).

This latter is the doctrine which inspires Carmelite teaching. John of the Cross insists that
small things may be obstacles to contemplative
love; Thérèse of Lisieux and Brother Lawrence
of the Resurrection rejoice in loving God
through the trivial affairs of daily life. The latter
discovered that "it is not necessary to have great
things to do. I turn my little omelette in the pan
for the love of God; when it is eaten, if I have
nothing to do, I prostrate myself on the ground
and adore my God, Who gave me the grace to
make it. Then I rise, more content than a king.
When I cannot do anything else, it is enough
for me to have lifted a straw from the earth for the
love of God."[18] His biographer touches the nerve
of this concept of self-abandonment when he
tells us: "His only means of going to God was
to do everything for love of him; he was indifferent whether he was occupied with one thing
or another, provided he did it for God. It was
God and not the thing that Brother considered.

[18] *Practice of the Presence of God*, p. 49.

149

He knew that the pettiness of the deed would not diminish the value of the offering because God needs nothing and considers in our works only the love that accompanies them."[19] Or as St. Thérèse of the Child Jesus put it: "it isn't that He wants us to do this or that; He wants us to love Him."

Nothing could be more instructive than to meditate on such words of these Carmelite saints, who encourage us to survey lovingly every slight detail of our daily lives, the smallest trifles, especially those that are obstacles on the way to perfection—our duties, our dealings with those about us—so that we may discover in them a thousand hidden chances to show God that we love Him.

Little Things as Reflections of God's Love

Little things as much as big ones are the work of God. "He has looked upon them as He went and He has clothed them in beauty,"[20] wrote St. John of the Cross. If we are to learn to love them,

[19] *Ibid.* p. 53.
[20] *Spiritual Canticle*, A, stanza 5.

FIDELITY IN LITTLE THINGS

not disdain them, we must view them from the standpoint of a child—that ecstatic and pure child's glance which can detect in things emanations of the divine, inhabiting them just as the sun's light dwells in the dew of a bright field at morning.

In this communion of all things in God, in this fraternity of little and great before his face, we achieve a sort of kingship over creation. We have already noted how Lawrence of the Resurrection "was more content than a king," even at his simple tasks in the kitchen. He thoroughly understood the meaning of small things and he knew how to find God in them. As his biographer tells us: "In all that he saw, in all that happened, he raised his heart at once, passing from the creature to the creator." And he cites one surprising example: "A tree that he noticed to be barren in winter made him immediately think of God and inspired in him so sublime a realization that forty years afterwards it was still as strong and vivid in his soul as when he had first received it."[21]

There are many wonderful stories about the love which Carmelite mystics had for nature. St.

[21] *Practice of the Presence of God*, xx p. 46.

Teresa tells us of the joy she felt in her hermitage because "from her bed she could see the river and the rising sun." And St. John of the Cross used to go to the top of the staircase in his monastery to watch the faery-like glow of dawn over the Alhambra. Perhaps the saints are sometimes thought to be too severe or too stiff in their approach to the world and nature; the very opposite is the case, since they love all things in and for God. But there is a place and a time for everything in their lives, and it is remarkable to note the flexibility with which they find it. Even St. Thérèse of the Child Jesus who practiced the most extreme forms of self-renunciation—to the extent of "developing a positive liking for ugly and inconvenient things" [22]—enjoyed some innocent distractions. She was not "disposed to be absolutely rigoristic about permissible satisfactions. Here, as otherwise, she conducted herself with singlemindedness, and she did not fail to bless God in his works. She liked to handle fruit, especially peaches, of which she admired the velvety softness; and she liked also to recognize the scents

[22] *Autobiography* p. 195.

of different flowers. She would have considered it a want of simplicity not to enjoy the things which drew her to God in love or in a sense of thankfulness—such as the charm of nature, of music, and of other delightful things."[23]

In the final analysis, our opportunities for loving God are a matter of our individual experiences and duties, particular occasions and encounters in our lives that do not exactly resemble those in the life of another. It is, nevertheless, true to say that for all of us things are what we make them, that by following the example of the saints, we can find ways to give our love of God its purest expression. With compelling spontaneity and adaptability our devotional lives will then deepen and extend themselves, particularly as we apply ourselves to the trivial details of our daily lives, searching out the opportunities to love God more and to find reflections of his surpassing love all around us.

---

[23] Père Petitot, *op. cit.*, p. 57, citing the text of the *processus* of her canonization.

If you enjoyed this book, you may be in-
terested in other volumes included in "The
Carmel Series on Christian Life." For free
catalogs and information, write the publisher:

DIMENSION BOOKS

P.O. BOX 21

WILKES-BARRE, PA.